ASWB

Masters Exam Practice Questions

ASWB Practice Tests & Review for the Association of Social Work Boards Exam

Dear Future Exam Success Story:

First of all, **THANK YOU** for purchasing Mometrix study materials!

Second, congratulations! You are one of the few determined test-takers who are committed to doing whatever it takes to excel on your exam. **You have come to the right place.** We developed these practice tests with one goal in mind: to deliver you the best possible approximation of the questions you will see on test day.

Standardized testing is one of the biggest obstacles on your road to success, which only increases the importance of doing well in the high-pressure, high-stakes environment of test day. Your results on this test could have a significant impact on your future, and these practice tests will give you the repetitions you need to build your familiarity and confidence with the test content and format to help you achieve your full potential on test day.

Your success is our success

We would love to hear from you! If you would like to share the story of your exam success or if you have any questions or comments in regard to our products, please contact us at **800-673-8175** or **support@mometrix.com**.

Thanks again for your business and we wish you continued success!

Sincerely,
The Mometrix Test Preparation Team

Written and edited by the Mometrix Exam Secrets Test Prep Team
Printed in the United States of America

TABLE OF CONTENTS

Practice Test #1

1. Executive functioning broadly refers to:

   a. the skill and capacity of a leader to lead.
   b. higher order cognitive functions and capacity.
   c. administrative policy and guidelines.
   d. a bureaucratic leadership style.

2. A patient who is described as "oriented times four" (or "oriented x4") is able to demonstrate awareness of which of the following four features?

   a. Name, date, city, and season
   b. Age, current year, location, and situation
   c. Name, gender, ethnicity, and marital status
   d. Person, place, time, and situation

3. A supervisor in a counseling clinic is approached by clerical staff asking how long they should retain patient counseling records. The BEST answer to could give is:

   a. until the client is no longer being seen.
   b. until the patient dies.
   c. until the statute of limitations expires.
   d. as long as possible, preferably indefinitely.

4. A social worker is called to evaluate a 64-year-old male with chronic obstructive pulmonary disease. He lives in an assisted living facility, and was brought to the emergency room by his daughter. She had taken him to lunch, and became distressed when he refused to return to the facility. He states he wants to live in his motor home, as he resents the loss of privacy at the facility. His daughter confirms he owns a working, fully self-contained motor home (i.e., stove, shower, refrigerator, etc.). He has adequate funds. He plans to park the motor home in a nearby Kampgrounds of America (KOA) campground, where all utilities can be hooked up. He can have food and other supplies delivered. However, it is November and it is unseasonably cold. The doctor confirms that the patient is prone to pneumonia, and the daughter states "he will die if he doesn't return to the facility." The patient refuses to consider any other living situation. In this situation, the social worker should:

   a. call the police and have them take the patient back to the facility.
   b. call adult protective services for further intervention.
   c. allow the patient to move into his motor home.
   d. place the patient on an involuntary hold for suicidal behavior.

5. A social worker is called to evaluate the 4-year-old child of a Southeast Asian family. The child has been ill for some days, and was brought to the emergency room with a temperature of 102° and symptoms of a pulmonary viral infection. During the medical examination, the physician noted numerous long, reddened welts on the child's skin, with superficial ecchymosis (bruising) and petechiae (minute hemorrhages) across the child's chest, suggestive of some form of abuse. Through an interpreter, he learned that a healing "shaman" had repeatedly performed a "coin rubbing" procedure in an attempt to draw out "bad wind" or "bad blood." The social worker views the child's back, and also see these marks. A nurse notes that "coin rubbing" to induce healing is common among traditional Vietnamese, Chinese, Hmong, Cambodians, and Laotians. She suggests that there is no need to report it as abuse. The social worker doesn't want to alienate the family or cause them to avoid seeking health care. As a social worker, the best response would be to:

a. concur with the nurse, and close the case.
b. call a local Southeast Asian cultural center to learn more.
c. call child protective services and let them decide.
d. call the police and request an investigation.

6. Define the terms reliability and validity in evaluative testing.

a. A test is reliable if it is easy to use, and valid if it is commonly used.
b. A test is reliable if it produces consistent results, and valid if it measures what it claims to measure.
c. A test is reliable if it includes Likert scale response options, and valid if it has been endorsed by major research institutions.
d. A test is reliable if it measures what it reports to measure, and valid if it produces consistent results.

7. A social worker has been seeing a significantly depressed client for some months and have been carefully keeping records following each session. Recently the client became upset, as he felt the social worker has been critical of his life and past decisions. During the last session, the client seemed overly suspicious and even a bit paranoid, despite efforts to reassure him and regain rapport. The next day, the client shows up without an appointment and demands to see the clinical notes. The social worker's BEST response would be to:

a. tell the client to make an appointment to review his records.
b. tell the client his is not permitted to see private notes.
c. immediately give the client a photocopy of his records.
d. give the client the original record, after making a copy.

8. A social worker has been called to see the family caregiver of a 32-year-old developmentally delayed dependent adult with a handprint bruise on his arm. The caregiver reports having to restrain the patient forcibly when the patient tried to leave the facility and run into busy traffic. The physician reports that the patient has no other old bruises, and no evidence of fear on the part of the patient when interacting with the caregiver is observed. The social worker realizes, however, that a report must be filed, due to the nature and circumstances surrounding the injury. After interviewing the caregiver and consulting with the physician, the physician tells the social worker that his nurse will be calling Adult Protective Services, so the social worker need not bother. The proper response is:

a. to thank the physician and nurse for taking on this burden.
b. to call APS later and make sure that they received the nurse's report.
c. to call the care facility's licensing board and make a report there.
d. to call Adult Protective Services yourself.

9. The typical time period of onset for a substance abuse disorder is during what ages?

a. Mid- to late adulthood
b. Late adulthood
c. Late adolescence to early adulthood
d. None of the above

10. A social worker has just had his first session with a 24-year-old college student. She is seeing him following the break-up of a two-year relationship, which occurred without warning about six weeks prior to this visit. As she explained it, "He met someone else and just moved on." She has been having trouble sleeping and concentrating on her studies since that time. Today she presents as dysphoric and tearful, but is affectively expressive and responsive to humor and other interactive stimuli. The university she attends is a considerable distance from her family and friends, leaving her with limited support during this difficult time. The most appropriate diagnosis would be:

a. primary insomnia.
b. major depression.
c. adjustment disorder with depressed mood.
d. acute stress disorder.

11. Identify the difference between psychotherapy and counseling.

a. Psychotherapy is generally considered to be long-term in nature, and counseling to be more short-term.
b. Psychotherapy uses a specific systems approach, while counseling is less bound by theory.
c. There is no difference between the two terms.
d. The term psychotherapy may only be used properly when referring to psychoanalysis.

12. In Erikson's psychosocial model of development, which stage is typical of those entering young adulthood?

a. Identify vs role confusion
b. Initiative vs guilt
c. Ego integrity vs despair
d. Intimacy vs isolation

13. Measuring the effectiveness of an intervention rather than the monetary savings is:

a. a cost-benefit analysis.
b. an efficacy study.
c. a product evaluation.
d. a cost-effective analysis.

14. What primary condition is treated by monoamine oxidase inhibitors (MAOIs), serotonin-norepinephrine reuptake inhibitors (SNRIs), and selective serotonin reuptake inhibitors (SSRIs)?

a. Attention deficit disorders
b. Eating disorders
c. Sleep disorders
d. Depressive disorders

15. A social worker works for a major corporation as a counselor. The available services are broad, and include family therapy and couples counseling. The social worker as sought out by a husband, experiencing significant marital discord. He is employed by the corporation, and he took the first steps to enter couples counseling. After a few sessions, it becomes clear that the wife has traits of a serious Axis II disorder, and over time the social worker begins seeing her exclusively. It has been two months since the last contact with the husband. The primary client is:

a. the husband.
b. the wife.
c. the corporation.
d. the couple.

16. There is a high co-morbidity rate between substance abuse and:

a. other disorders.
b. yearly income.
c. IQ.
d. none of the above.

17. All of the following are National Association of Social Workers (NASW) standards for cultural competence EXCEPT:

a. social workers should endeavor to seek out, employ, and retain employees who provide diversity in the profession.
b. social workers shall endeavor to resources and services in the native language of those they serve, including the use of translated materials and interpreters.
c. social workers should develop the skills to work with clients in culturally competent ways, and with respect for diversity.
d. social workers should work with diverse clients only if they have had specific training in that client's unique cultural background.

18. The Health Insurance Portability and Accountability Act (HIPAA) regulates:

a. the transfer of patients from one facility to another.
b. the rights of the individual related to privacy of health information.
c. medical trials.
d. workplace safety.

19. A social worker is working with a 42-year-old executive who is coping with the after-effects of a business failure and subsequent personal bankruptcy. He is generally coping well, but he reveals a past history of alcoholism and indicates that he is struggling with a desire to resume drinking. The social worker encourages him to follow with an Alcoholics Anonymous group, but he responds that he thinks he can manage without such help. The social worker has a personal drinking history herself, and she recognizes the warning signs. She then considers revealing her personal story to bolster her recommendation that he seek help, and to demonstrate the level of her personal understanding and empathy, and to motivate him to take further action. The BEST course of action would be:

a. to withhold this information, because it involves personal disclosure by a social worker in a professional counseling relationship.
b. to share the personal story, because it is entirely relevant to the client's specific situation.
c. to share the personal story, because the consequences if the client returns to drinking are potentially severe.
d. to disclose limited information, being careful not to reveal too much about one's own history, in order to motivate the client.

20. The core features of borderline personality disorder are often disagreed upon. However, two factors are common to the disorder—highly variable mood and:

a. delusions
b. impulsive behavior
c. hallucinations
d. psychotic ideology

21. Cultural competence in individual social work practice is best defined as:

a. the ability to work well with diverse groups.
b. receiving excellent training in diversity.
c. the possession of a wide-ranging knowledge of many diverse groups.
d. the ability to recognize stereotypes, prejudiced views, and biases.

22. A retrospective attempt to determine the cause of an event is:

a. root cause analysis.
b. external benchmarking.
c. internal trending.
d. tracer methodology.

23. A study attempts to measure the efficacy of a new antidepressant medication. A "control" group of depression sufferers will receive only a placebo, while an "intervention" group will receive the new medication. In this study, the "null hypothesis" would state the following:

a. the intervention group will report fewer symptoms of depression than the control group.
b. the control group will report fewer symptoms of depression than the intervention group.
c. both the control group and the intervention group will report fewer numbers of depressive symptoms.
d. there shall be no measurable difference in depression symptom reporting between the control group and the intervention group.

24. In adults, manic episodes last for how long?

a. A few hours
b. At least 2 days
c. At least one week
d. At least 3 months

25. A manic episode first experienced after the age of 40 is:

a. common.
b. highly unusual.
c. unlikely to be due to substance abuse.
d. unlikely to be due to a medical condition.

26. Basing one's feelings, attitudes, and beliefs regarding a specific group of people upon preconceived ideas, rumors, and inferences is BEST defined as:

a. bias.
b. prejudice.
c. stereotyping.
d. singling out.

27. Clinical pathways should be based on:

a. a survey of current practices in the area.
b. committee recommendations.
c. evidence-based research.
d. staff preferences.

28. In statistical research, a "Type I Error" (also called an "alpha error," or a "false positive") refers to:

a. failing to reject the null hypothesis when the null hypothesis is false.
b. a failure to randomize research participants, thereby potentially introducing bias.
c. rejecting the null hypothesis when the null hypothesis is true.
d. assuming a normal statistical distribution when it is skewed.

29. An 80-year old patient is dying of cancer and has been in and out of consciousness. The family should be encouraged to:

a. go home, as the patient does not know they are present.
b. talk to the patient, as hearing is usually the last sense to fail.
c. offer the patient frequent sips of water to avoid dehydration.
d. raise the head of the patient's bed if respirations become rattling to help the patient clear secretions.

30. Bipolar disorder can easily be confused with which of the following disorders?

a. Borderline personality disorder
b. Clinical depression
c. Anxiety disorder
d. Conduct disorder

31. Categories of risk for early-onset intellectual disability include which of the following?

a. Problems at birth
b. Poverty
c. Age of verbal acquisition
d. Problems at birth and poverty

32. In statistical research, a "Type II Error" (also called a "beta error" or "false negative") refers to:

a. a failure to reject the null hypothesis when the null hypothesis is false.
b. erroneously selecting a statistical analysis model based upon invalid assumptions.
c. rejecting the null hypothesis when the null hypothesis is true.
d. making an error in mathematical calculations, upon which a finding is based.

33. ______________ is a disorder of thought, unlike ______________ which is a disorder of mood.

a. Borderline; conduct disorder
b. Conduct disorder; depression
c. Bipolar disorder; schizophrenia
d. Schizophrenia; bipolar disorder

34. Basing the opportunities, options, and benefits available to a specific group of people based upon preconceptions and assumptions is BEST defined as:

a. bigotry.
b. discrimination.
c. prejudice.
d. misogyny.

35. Failure mode and effects analysis (FMEA) is done:

a. retrospectively.
b. upon utilization of a new process.
c. during the trial of a new process.
d. prior to utilization of a new process.

36. How do team members usually deal with issues of power?

a. By observing and emulating the leader
b. By arguing
c. By following strict rules of discourse
d. By rotating leadership roles

37. A social worker is hired by a private practice therapist who operates a court-supervised violent offender treatment program. One of the social worker's responsibilities is to screen new client referrals, to ensure that only low-risk, first-time offenders are accepted into the program. In this process, the social worker is to have each client sign a treatment consent form, which also includes a detailed consent for release of information. The worker notes that instead of the usual time and target limits, the form allows information to be released at any time to "any law enforcement agency," "any spouse, ex-spouse, or significant other," "any welfare or abuse protection agency," etc. When asking about the ethics of having clients sign this form, the social worker is told, "It's a hassle to try and get specific information releases, and the safety of the public is at stake. Use the form." The BEST response is to:

a. use the form as directed.
b. refuse to use the form.
c. call the licensing board and discuss the form.
d. call law enforcement and discuss the form.

38. Which assessment tool for dementia involves remembering and repeating the names of 3 common objects and drawing the face of a clock with all 12 numbers and hands indicating the time specified by the examiner?

a. Mini-mental state exam (MMSE)
b. Mini-cog
c. Digit Repetition Test
d. Confusion Assessment Method

39. Identify the four most common minority classifications:

a. ethnicity, gender, sexual orientation, culture.
b. religion, race, gender, sexual orientation.
c. age, appearance, social standing, gender.
d. age, gender, race, sexual orientation.

40. A client reports his fear of the local television station and his belief that it is transmitting harmful sound waves. What he's likely experiencing would be called a:

a. hallucination.
b. delusion.
c. somatic hallucination.
d. gustatory delusion.

41. The term "deinstitutionalization" refers to:

a. helping a client accommodate to a community living environment after having been institutionalized for an extended period (usually, years).
b. creating a treatment program that serves the needs of the client, as opposed to the needs of the institution.
c. changes in policy and law that led to the release of many mental health patients who would have otherwise remained in institutional settings.
d. a philosophy of client- social worker collaboration in treatment, as opposed to hierarchical social worker-driven treatment.

42. Thought insertion/withdrawal refers to what?

a. A psychoanalytic therapy technique
b. The belief that thoughts are being put into or taken out of one's head
c. A behavior therapy technique related to operant conditioning
d. A type of hallucination

43. The Occupational Safety and Health Administration (OSHA) regulates:

a. patient right to privacy.
b. disposal methods for sharps, such as needles.
c. reimbursement for services.
d. patient surveys.

44. A disease characterized by a diffuse atrophy of the brain is:

a. bipolar disorder.
b. Alzheimer's disease.
c. schizoaffective disorder.
d. obsessive compulsive disorder.

45. According to Bush et al (2003), what percentage of people who successfully commit suicide have made a prior attempt?

a. 76%
b. 23%
c. 49%
d. less than 10%

46. Which scale is used to assess and predict the risk of a patient developing pressure sores based upon sensory perception, moisture, activity, mobility, nutrition pattern, and friction and sheer?

a. Norton Scale
b. Pressure Ulcer Scale for Healing (PUSH)
c. The Braden Scale
d. Diabetic Foot Ulcer Scale (DFS)

47. A primary purpose of interdisciplinary teams is:

a. sharing ideas and perspectives to solve problems.
b. cost-savings.
c. improved patient satisfaction.
d. time saving.

48. The belief that one's personal background (i.e., race, culture, religion, etc.) is superior to that of others is known as:

a. stereotypy.
b. racism.
c. ethnocentrism.
d. elitism.

49. A 60-year old male is being treated for a myocardial infarction. While he is progressing well physically, he becomes upset when asked to make independent decisions and he rings the call bell constantly asking for reassurance that he will get well. This psychological response to stress is an example of:

a. dependence.
b. passivity.
c. depression.
d. confusion.

50. In terms of quality assurance in social work practice, what does the acronym "CQI" represent?

a. Certification of Quality Institute
b. Communication Quality Index
c. Command of Quality Indicators
d. Continuous Quality Improvement

51. Which members of the healthcare institution are responsible for identifying performance improvement projects?

a. Administrative staff
b. Nursing team leaders
c. Physicians
d. All staff

52. Identify the five classifications of race most commonly used.

a. Asian, Black, Hispanic, Native American, White.
b. Asian, Black, Native American, Spanish, White.
c. African, Asian, Indian, Spanish, White.
d. Asian, Black, Mexican, Native American, White.

53. Which type of sexual disorder is most likely to come to the attention of a social worker?

a. Gender identity disorder
b. Voyeurism
c. Paraphilia
d. Sexual function disorders

54. Which of the following is part of 12 leading health indicators (determinants of health) outlined in Healthy People 2020?

a. Pregnancy
b. Chronic disease
c. Environmental quality
d. Family support

55. Identify the missing step in Albert R. Roberts seven-stage crisis intervention model: 1) assess lethality; 2) establish rapport; 3) ________; 4) deal with feelings; 5) explore alternatives; 6) develop an action plan; 7) follow-up. The third step is:

a. evaluate resources.
b. identify problems.
c. environmental control.
d. collateral contacts.

56. Which of the following provides research and funding for the development of evidence-based practice guidelines?

a. Occupational Health and Safety Association (OSHA)
b. Food and Drug Administration (FDA)
c. Health Insurance Portability and Accountability Act (HIPAA)
d. Agency for Healthcare Research and Quality (AHRQ)

57. Frotteuristic disorder refers to a:

a. personality disorder.
b. symptom of schizophrenia.
c. sexual disorder.
d. common bipolar symptom.

58. Presenting symptoms that may appear to reflect from mental illness, but which actually arise from specific cultural practices, beliefs, or values, are referred to as:

a. belief-based symptoms.
b. iatrogenic symptoms.
c. factitious syndromes.
d. culture-bound syndromes.

59. According to principles of adult learning, adult learners tend to be:

a. unmotivated.
b. lacking in self-direction.
c. practical and goal-oriented.
d. insecure.

60. The Instrumental Activities of Daily Living (IADL) tool includes an assessment of:

a. bathing.
b. toileting.
c. ascending or descending stairs.
d. financial responsibility.

61. Which of the following has criteria for diagnosis that it occurs for at least two years, more days than not, making it not very episodic?

a. Bipolar disorder
b. Disruptive mood dysregulation disorder
c. Major depressive disorder
d. Dysthymic disorder

62. Which is the most common lifetime disorder?

a. Conduct disorder
b. Depression
c. Borderline personality disorder
d. Schizophrenia

63. In obtaining an interpreter for a non–English-speaking client, the best option would be to select:

a. another staff person at the facility or agency.
b. a professional interpreter.
c. a friend of the client.
d. a relative of the client.

64. The best time to initiate conflict resolution is:

a. when those in conflict have had time to resolve their differences.
b. when conflict first emerges.
c. when conflict interferes with function.
d. when those involved ask for conflict resolution.

65. The psychological theory that characterizes a hierarchy of needs culminating in self-actualization was developed by:

a. Jung.
b. Havighurst.
c. Maslow.
d. Freud.

66. According to J.W. Drisko (2009), the five key factors required for a quality therapeutic relationship between client and clinician are: 1) affective attunement; 2) mutual affirmation; 3) joint efforts to resolve missteps; 4) ________; and 5) using varying types of empathy. The fourth key factor is:

a. use of humor.
b. accepting criticism.
c. capacity to trust.
d. goal congruence.

67. Certain exceptions to confidentiality exist. These include: 1) mandated reporting issues; 2) subpoenas or other court orders; 3) treatment continuity (cross-coverage by other agency staff); and all of the following EXCEPT:

a. disclosures for insurance coverage purposes.
b. disclosures at a client's written request.
c. disclosures to an employer providing insurance coverage.
d. disclosures regarding a child (e.g., mandated reporting, violations of the law, etc.).

68. Upon first meeting a client, a social worker should begin by taking the following steps (in the order listed):

a. summarize legal and ethical obligations, complete a counseling contract, explore the client's presenting problem, and assess the client.
b. complete a service contract, summarize legal and ethical obligations.
c. establish rapport, summarize legal and ethical obligations, complete a service contract, and assess the client.
d. assess the client, summarize legal and ethical obligations, complete a service contract, and establish a rapport.

69. Which of the following theories is characterized by the contention that life is an unending process of changes and transitions?

a. Life course/Life span
b. Modernization
c. Geo-transcendence
d. Exchange

70. An organization that is arranged hierarchically, with numerous departments and units through which segments of specialized services are provided, moving toward the achievement of a common goal, is referred to as a(n):

a. complex organization.
b. hierarchical organization.
c. bureaucracy.
d. institution.

71. A woman describes herself as happily married, yet she occasionally engages in episodic sexual contacts with other men. When asked what motivates her episodes of infidelity, she provides a rather vague initial response and finally states, "I guess I just don't know." According to Freud, what area of cognition is involved in her behavior?

a. the subconscious mind.
b. the preconscious mind.
c. the conscious mind.
d. the unconscious mind.

72. When considering outcome measures, striving for patient satisfaction is:

a. a long-term outcome.
b. a short-term outcome.
c. both a long-term and a short-term outcome.
d. a process.

73. A form of client assessment that focuses on a client's social and relational functioning is known as:

a. a genogram.
b. a social status examination.
c. a social resource review.
d. a social assessment report.

74. Which of the following can increase one's risk of attempting suicide in the future?

a. Prior suicide ideation
b. Past suicidal behavior in one's family
c. History of frequent mobility
d. All of the above

75. Assessing a client by means of a checklist or questionnaire is particularly useful when:

a. the client doesn't want to see the social worker.
b. the client is unsure how to describe the situation, or if it is complex or risk laden and the social worker needs to be thorough.
c. the social worker is too busy to see the client personally.
d. the social worker wishes to avoid a client interview.

76. When considering the use of an interpreter for a patient who does not speak English, which consideration is most important?

a. The interpreter has training in medical vocabulary for both languages
b. The interpreter speaks both languages well
c. The interpreter knows the patient's history
d. The interpreter is available onsite

77. Freud described the concept of pain (whether physical or emotional) as arising through the psychic process of:

a. repression.
b. introjection.
c. cathexis.
d. fixation.

78. The basic functions of administrators include: 1) monitoring, reviewing, advising, and evaluating employees; 2) planning and delegation; and all of the following EXCEPT:

a. frontline organizational services.
b. advocacy (both horizontally with departmental staff, and vertically between other departments and staff).
c. conflict resolution and mediation.
d. planning and delegation.

79. A diagram that helps individual and families to visually depict the quality of individual and/or family relationships with others, within a community, and with important resources in their lives (e.g., food, shelter, work, school, health care, etc.) is called:

a. an eco-map.
b. a family diagram.
c. a genomap.
d. a relational diagram.

80. A 40-year-old client presents with complaints regarding not feeling comfortable socially. He states that after gaining weight he now finds social situations to be overwhelming. He has stopped attending church and recreational activities, and does not engage in new activities, although before he was known for being adventurous. A likely diagnosis would be:

a. borderline personality disorder.
b. avoidant personality disorder.
c. schizotypal personality disorder.
d. depressive disorder.

81. The DSM-5 provides for the diagnosis of specific personality disorders and one category for indeterminate behaviors that appear to be characteristic of a personality disorder. These disorders are grouped into clusters. Identify the cluster that does not properly describe a personality disorder group:

a. Cluster A: paranoid, schizoid, and schizotypal disorders (also referred to as "odd or eccentric behavior disorders").
b. Cluster B: impulsivity and/or affective dysregulation disorders (also referred to as "dramatic, emotional, or erratic disorders").
c. Cluster C: anxiety and compulsive disorders (also referred to as "anxious or fearful disorders").
d. Cluster D: violent and/or explosive disorders (also referred to as "aggressive and intrusive conduct disorders").

82. A social worker meets with a client who has been struggling financially. It becomes apparent that he must reduce his standard of living in order to maintain financial solvency. He therefore sells his large luxury automobile and purchases a small but reliable economy vehicle, realizing considerable savings. According to Heinz Hartmann's "Ego Psychology" this kind of accommodation is an example of:

a. defensive functioning.
b. alloplastic behavior.
c. integrative functioning.
d. autoplastic behavior.

83. Which of the following professional communication skills is used to facilitate communication with intra- and inter-disciplinary teams?

a. Interpreting the statements of others to facilitate the flow of ideas
b. Reacting and responding to facts rather than feelings
c. Providing advice when it appears needed
d. Asking questions to challenge other people's ideas

84. Identify the most commonly used intelligence measurement scale:

a. Wechsler-Bellevue Intelligence Scale.
b. Stanford-Binet Intelligence Scale.
c. Binet-Simon Intelligence Scale.
d. Wechsler Adult Intelligence Scale.

85. A supervisor's role involves: 1) being a role model; 2) recruitment and orientation; 3) day-to-day management; 4) staff training, education, and development; 5) staff assessments and reviews; and all of the following EXCEPT:

a. advocating for staff and program needs.
b. allocating interdepartmental operating funds.
c. evaluating the program for ongoing improvement.
d. providing support and counsel to staff.

86. Certain codes in DSM-5 are used to identify conditions that are a focus of clinical attention, but for which insufficient information exists to determine if the issues can be attributed to a mental disorder (or which may, in fact, not be due to a mental disorder but still require clinical attention). These codes are called:

a. DSM-5 Codes.
b. GAF Codes.
c. V Codes.
d. ICD Codes.

87. According to "Object Relations Theory," an infant's separation and individuation from its mother should largely be complete by the time the infant is aged:

a. 24 months.
b. Five months.
c. 14 months.
d. Nine months.

88. All of the following are methods of program evaluation EXCEPT:

a. outcome evaluation.
b. participatory evaluation.
c. reciprocal evaluation.
d. process-oriented evaluation.

89. The update to the Diagnostic and Statistical Manual of Mental Disorders (DSM)-5 included major changes to categories and classifications. Which of the following is not a DSM-5 category?

a. Sleep-wake disorders
b. Sexual dysfunctions
c. Pervasive developmental disorders
d. Gender dysphoria

90. A client comes to see a social worker with numerous personal issues of varying severity. The decision regarding the issue(s) that should be addressed first should be made:

a. by the client alone.
b. by the client, in exploration with the social worker.
c. by the social worker alone.
d. based upon severity of life impact.

91. The following are all approaches to program "outcome evaluation" EXCEPT:

a. the aggregate evaluation approach.
b. the decision-oriented approach.
c. the experimental evaluation approach.
d. the performance audit approach.

92. Self-Psychology, as postulated by Heinz Kohut, acknowledges that personality is partly formed by social structure. A cohesive self is achieved by incorporating the perceptions and functions of healthy significant others and objects into an internalized self structure through a process called:

a. empathic mirroring.
b. rapprochement.
c. differentiation.
d. transmuting internalization.

93. A social worker has been seeing a client for several weeks, with considerable progress having been made. As a mutually agreed upon date for termination approaches, the client expresses considerable anxiety and even some anger regarding the impending termination. The social worker's best initial response would be to do which of the following?

a. Offer a follow-up appointment some weeks away
b. Assure the client that services can again be sought at any time
c. Cancel the termination date and continue services
d. Explore and discuss the client's feelings about termination

94. A client verbalizes discontent regarding the progress of his treatment plan. The social worker asks, "Are you saying you're not pleased with your progress up to this point?" The social worker then adds, "You sound upset" and reassures the client that "things will get better soon." This communication involves several errors. Which of the following is one of them?

a. A lack of demonstrated warmth and empathy on the part of the social worker
b. A response that isn't confrontational enough
c. Inappropriate reassurance
d. A focus on conscious thoughts

95. The following are all approaches to program "participatory evaluation" EXCEPT:

a. cluster evaluations.
b. action research.
c. self evaluations.
d. peer reviews.

96. According the DSM-5 criteria, a client that has previously met the criteria for stimulant use disorder but now has not met the criteria for stimulant use in 10 months (except for craving) would be termed to be in _____ remission.

a. Full
b. Partial
c. Early
d. Sustained

97. The following are all comparisons between consultation and supervision EXCEPT:

a. consultation is provided by an outside expert, while supervision is provided by an internal staff leader.
b. consultants have broad administrative authority, while supervisors have only interdepartmental authority.
c. consultants provide advice and recommendations, while supervisors tend to provide binding directives and procedures.
d. consultation is episodic (as sought) and voluntary, while supervision is ongoing and mandatory.

98. The primary focus of Gestalt Psychology, as founded by Frederick Perls, is on:

a. the developmental issues and the past, as they influence the present.
b. the "here and now."
c. adaptation and the future.
d. moral development.

99. A 19 year old college student sustains a severe head injury in an accident. Post-rehab testing reveals a subsequent IQ of 62. Which diagnosis would be the most likely?

a. Dementia, mild, due to head trauma
b. Mild neurocognitive disorder due to traumatic brain injury
c. Borderline intellectual functioning
d. Intellectual disability, mild, due to head trauma

100. The process by which a client and social worker review past goals, summarize progress made, and finalize plans to maintain and continue past progress is called:

a. closure.
b. wrap-up.
c. finalization.
d. termination.

101. A type of record-keeping that consolidates and reports all information (including progress, interventions, and conclusions) in an ongoing story form is called:

a. descriptive recording.
b. journaling.
c. narrative recording.
d. summary recording.

102. A single mother and a teenage son present for relationship problems. The son is actively defiant of instructions, argues regularly over minor requests, and can be spiteful and resentful over normal parenting efforts. School performance is marginal, but only one unexcused absence has occurred during the current school year, which is nearing its end. The most appropriate diagnosis would be:

a. oppositional defiant disorder
b. conduct disorder
c. intermittent explosive disorder
d. parent-child relational problem

103. According to Erik Erikson's model of the Psychosocial Stages of Development, individuals over the age of 50 are moving into the following stage:

a. ego integrity versus despair.
b. intimacy versus isolation.
c. identity versus role confusion.
d. generativity versus stagnation.

104. A type of record-keeping that chronologically and systematically records client information (usually beginning with a fact-laden face sheet, a statement of the presenting problem, goals, and current obstacles) is called:

a. outline recording.
b. summary recording.
c. contiguous recording.
d. process recording.

105. According to the DSM-5, a client with an intelligence quotient (IQ) of 59, who lives alone but requires support to do grocery shopping and manage money, is unable to read and is very gullible should be considered to have:

a. moderate mental retardation
b. borderline intellectual functioning
c. moderate intellectual disability
d. mild intellectual disability

106. An elderly female client presents with marked disorientation, word-finding problems, memory impairment, and a high degree of distractibility. Her daughter states that the patient was "just fine" until two days prior to this contact, and that she seems better in the mornings. There have been no external or environmental changes. The most likely diagnosis would be:

a. medication-induced cognitive changes
b. senile dementia, rapid onset
c. delirium
d. neurocognitive disorder, not otherwise specified

107. Another type of record-keeping focuses on goals, and is segmented into four sections: 1) factual information (a face sheet or database section); 2) the assessment and expected treatment plan; 3) the progress notes; and 4) progress review entries (usually at 6-12 week intervals). It is called:

a. person-oriented recording.
b. goal-oriented recording.
c. manifold recording.
d. continuous review recording.

108. The capacity to understand death is a developmental process. From ages 2-5, death is not understood as permanent and may be viewed as sleep. From ages 5-9, death's permanence may be recognized, but some children may not understand it will happen to them (external symbols such as angels and skeletons predominate). By age ten (but more often around age seven, especially if loss of a pet or loved one has occurred), death is understood as permanent, irreversible, and inevitable. The two developmental stages that encompass these increasingly elaborate understandings (in ascending order), as identified by Piaget, are:

a. formal operational, concrete operational.
b. pre-operational, formal operational.
c. pre-operational, concrete operational.
d. sensorimotor, pre-operational.

109. A husband and wife present for help with her substance use. She had been recreationally using cocaine on some weekends, and indicates that she has a strong desire to stop, but has been unsuccessful in stopping before. The precipitating incident was an episode of driving under the influence on a weeknight that resulted in her arrest, impounding of the family car, and considerable fines, charges, and increases in automobile insurance. This is the second driving incident in the last two years. The most appropriate diagnosis for the wife, given the relevant details would be:

a. stimulant intoxication.
b. stimulant dependence.
c. stimulant use disorder.
d. stimulant use withdrawal.

110. A social worker is seeing a 16-year-old youth who has, for the past year, been losing his temper frequently, is regularly argumentative with adults, often refuses to follow direct requests, is easily annoyed, and routinely uses blaming to escape responsibility. Approximately four months ago he was caught in a single episode of shoplifting. The most appropriate diagnosis for this youth is:

a. oppositional defiant disorder.
b. conduct disorder.
c. intermittent explosive disorder
d. antisocial personality disorder

111. An additional type of record-keeping focuses largely on a client's ongoing issues. It contains four components: 1) factual information (a face sheet or database section); 2) a checklist section providing a rank-order roster of client issues; 3) a resolution plan (steps for resolving the primary issues); and 4) progress notes summarizing actions taken and results achieved. This method of record-keeping was borrowed from the medical arena, and is modeled after the "SOAP" format (subjective, objective, assessment, and plan). In social work it is called:

a. transactional recording.
b. problem-oriented recording.
c. summary recording.
d. SOAP recording.

112. An early cognitive theorist, who worked directly with Freud, established a theoretical orientation that differed from Freud's in three key features: 1) an individual's personality is best perceived as a whole, rather than as having hierarchical segments or parts; 2) social relationships drive behavior more than sexual motivations; and 3) current beliefs and thoughts play a far greater role in human behavior than is suggested via psychoanalytic theory, which is based largely in the unconscious and in past experiences and beliefs. The name of this theorist is:

a. Lawrence Kohlberg.
b. Anna Freud.
c. Albert Ellis.
d. Alfred Adler.

113. A 20-year-old male college student has been referred for evaluation by his family. They note that over the last six to seven months he has increasingly avoided contact and/or talking with family members and friends, that he often seems intensely preoccupied, and that his hygiene and grooming have become very poor. In speaking with him, the social worker notes that he seems very guarded, that his affect is virtually expressionless, and that he resists talking. After he is coaxed to speak, his speech is very tangential, disorganized, and even incoherent at times. He seems to be responding to internal stimuli (hallucinations and/or intrusive thoughts). The family and he deny substance abuse. Which would be the MOST likely diagnosis?

a. Schizophrenia
b. Somatization disorder
c. Bipolar disorder
d. Major depression with psychotic features

114. The two major classifications of research are:

a. statistical and descriptive.
b. numerical and narrative.
c. quantitative and qualitative.
d. pragmatic and theoretical.

115. Encopresis is defined as:

a. the voluntary or involuntary passage of stool in an inappropriate place by a child over the age of four.
b. the voluntary or involuntary passage of stool in an inappropriate place by a competent adult.
c. deliberate fecal incontinence only in a child over age four.
d. involuntary fecal incontinence only in a developmentally delayed adult.

116. Critical components of universal precaution practice standards of the Occupational Safety and Health Administration include which of the following?

a. Use of personal protective barriers
b. Proper hand washing
c. Precautions in handling sharps
d. All of the above

117. Common forms of research designs include all of the following EXCEPT:

a. descriptive studies.
b. experimental studies.
c. exploratory studies.
d. statistical studies.

118. Which cognitive-behavior approach incorporates a theory of emotion known as the "ABC Theory of Emotion"?

a. mindfulness-based cognitive therapy.
b. rational emotive therapy.
c. functional analytic psychotherapy.
d. cognitive analytic therapy.

119. Following a recent remarriage, a blended family has sought help from a social worker. They are struggling to develop workable family roles, standards, and cohesion. Following considerable effort, the family begins to work together better and conflicts have been largely minimized. According to eco-systems theory, the changes would best be referred to as:

a. socialization
b. adaptation
c. role reorganization
d. social accommodation

120. The following criteria are all used to distinguish delirium from dementia, except one. Select the pair that is not used to distinguish delirium from dementia:

a. acute onset vs slow onset.
b. diagnosis in patients under age 65 vs patients over age 65.
c. consciousness fluctuates broadly vs relatively stable symptoms.
d. global cognitive impairments vs idiosyncratic cognitive impairments.

121. Problem identification, background information, hypothesis formulation, operationalization (selecting a study model and data collection), evaluation (data analysis), and further theorization can be referred to as:

a. study design.
b. the research process.
c. scientific investigation.
d. knowledge generation.

122. A 22-year old college student comes to a hospital emergency room complaining of chest pain. The medical work-up is negative. The social worker learns that his father recently died of a heart attack (a few weeks ago) while he was away at school, and that he is now experiencing episodes of sudden-onset fear accompanied by symptoms such as a rapid heart rate, sweating, tremors, chest pain, and shortness of breath, and feelings that he is about to die. After a short time the symptoms subside. In recent days he has been sleeping outside the hospital, fearful that he may not otherwise arrive in time when the symptoms strike. Which is the most likely diagnosis?

a. Generalized anxiety disorder
b. Panic disorder
c. Somatization disorder
d. Post-traumatic stress disorder

123. In working with a client, the social worker becomes aware that she persistently behaves in ways to please or gain the approval of others. While this is not always problematic, the social worker discovers that she is obsessed with wearing the "right" clothes, living in the "right" neighborhood, and marrying the "right" person. At present, her finances are in a shambles as she tries desperately to "keep up with the Joneses," and her romantic life is suffering, as she only pursues relations that she believes others think are optimum, rather than judging relationships on more personally relevant values, such as her feelings for them, baseline compatibility, etc. Utilizing Kohlberg's Theory of Moral Development, specify the Level and Stage of moral development that applies to this individual:

a. conventional Level, Stage 3.
b. pre-conventional Level, Stage 1.
c. post-conventional Level, Stage 6.
d. conventional Level, Stage 4.

124. "Single system" research designs involve observing one client or system only (n=1) before, during, and after an intervention. Because of their flexibility and capacity to measure change over time, single system designs are frequently used by practitioners to evaluate:

a. their practice.
b. difficult clients.
c. conformation to policy.
d. regulation adherence.

125. A social worker is seeing a client who has previously been diagnosed with heroin use disorder. He has not met the criteria for substance use disorder, except for craving, for 5 months. He lives at his mother's home and is using a methadone treatment program. He would be classified as:

a. early remission.
b. sustained remission.
c. not in remission.
d. early remission, controlled environment.

126. Bipolar disorder is most commonly treated with which of the following medication?

a. lithium
b. haloperidol
c. librium
d. prozac

127. Name the four kinds of reinforcement used in Operant Conditioning Theory, as established by B.F. Skinner:

a. positive reinforcement, conditioned stimulus, consequence responses, and negative reinforcement.
b. negative reinforcement, punishment, conditioned responses, and antecedent events.
c. consequence responses, deprivation responses, rewards, time-out responses.
d. positive reinforcement, negative reinforcement, punishment, and extinction.

128. There are three types of single system research "case studies" or "pre-designs." Identify the answer below that is ERRONEOUSLY described.

a. Changes in case study (Design B-C).
b. Intervention only (Design B).
c. Observation only (Design A).
d. Time series only (Design A-B).

129. To meet criteria for diagnosis of schizophrenia a client must have at least two out of three major symptoms for a significant amount of time during a one month interval. Which of the following is NOT one of the three major symptoms <u>necessary</u> to diagnosis schizophrenia?

a. Delusions
b. Hallucinations
c. Disorganized speech
d. Blunted affect

130. A 48-year old woman is seen in clinic for personal problems. Upon interview she describes having quit her grocery clerk job because of fear that something might happen that she can't cope with at the work site. When pressed, she is vague but finally states that she's fearful she could have gas (burping or flatulence), bowel or bladder incontinence, or be badly embarrassed by others on the job. She acknowledges that she has no current gaseous or incontinence issues, and that she's never been humiliated by anyone in the past. However, she insists that she cannot tolerate the possibility it might occur. The most likely diagnosis is:

a. Panic disorder.
b. Agoraphobia.
c. Social anxiety disorder.
d. General anxiety disorder.

131. Identify the four steps (in the proper order) that Albert Bandura formulated to operationalize Social Learning Theory:

a. Attention, retention, reproduction, motivation.
b. Attention, motivation, retention, reproduction.
c. Motivation, retention, reproduction, attention.
d. Reproduction, motivation, attention, retention.

132. In an "A-B" single system research design, "A" indicates an initial phase without any intervention, and "B" refers to the intervention phase and requisite data collection. This design is called:

a. The "intervention" single system design.
b. The "planned" single system design.
c. The "basic" single system design.
d. The "descriptive" single system design.

133. As part of a pending disability application, a social worker meets with the client. The client voices complaints about significant chronic back and shoulder pain, which is the basis of the claim. During the course of the in-home assessment the social worker notes that the individual is able to bend down to move and pick things up, and is able to reach over her head into an upper cabinet—all without apparent difficulty or complaints of pain. The most appropriate determination would be:

a. Illness anxiety disorder.
b. Malingering.
c. Factitious disorder.
d. Somatic symptom disorder.

134. A couple presenting for counseling evaluation reveals that the wife comes from a dysfunctional, neglectful, alcoholic home and has little trust or tolerance for relationships. Consequently, their marriage is marred by constant arguing and distrust, frequent demands that he leave, episodes of impulsive violence, alternating with brief periods of excessive over-valuation (stating that he is the "best thing that ever happened" to her, "too good" for her, et cetera. Which is the most likely diagnosis?

a. Anti-social personality disorder
b. Histrionic personality disorder
c. Borderline personality disorder
d. Narcissistic personality disorder

135. A social worker has a client experiencing significant cognitive dissonance. She considers herself as a very principled person, and holds herself to very high standards of conduct. She very openly condemns drinking, gambling, and other "vices," yet she reveals that she has long struggled with a desire to gamble. Her very vigorous denunciations of gambling, even while harboring a desire herself, constitute the application of what defense mechanism?

a. Projection
b. Rationalization
c. Reaction formation
d. Substitution

136. A social worker should choose a practice framework based upon any of the following criteria EXCEPT:

a. an accepted psychological theoretical base.
b. treatment goals and treatment type (individual, family, group, etc.).
c. the model most commonly used by other social workers.
d. the client's problem and/or time and resources available.

137. There are four categories of measurement. One is called the "nominal" category. Nominal measurements are used when two or more "named" variables exist (e.g., male/female, high/medium/low, etc.). All of the following are also categories of measurement, EXCEPT:

a. the "interval" category.
b. the "additive" category.
c. the "ordinal" category.
d. the "ratio" category.

138. Which one of the following does NOT represent common practice frameworks?

a. Ethnic-sensitive and feminist frameworks
b. Systems and eco-system frameworks
c. Generalist and strengths frameworks
d. Behavioral and cognitive frameworks

139. A social worker has been contacted by a couple to assist them with issues of marital discord. They have been married about six months. The wife presents as vulnerable, tearful, and anxious, and the husband presents as angry and overwhelmed. The wife openly claims that "he has never loved me," and expresses anger that he married her without "the proper feelings." The husband responds that he has "done everything possible" to "prove" his love (to the point of near bankruptcy and jeopardizing his employment with frequent absences), but nothing is sufficient. During the interview, the social worker discovers that she has had many short-term relationships in the past, that she has a history of suicide gestures and "fits of rage." Further, she frequently demands a divorce and then begs him to stay, is routinely physically assaultive, etc. The most likely diagnosis is:

a. intermittent explosive disorder.
b. histrionic personality disorder.
c. paranoid personality disorder.
d. borderline personality disorder.

140. A newly divorced client has been working on numerous past marital issues, and was readily disclosing many feelings and concerns. However, when episodes of her infidelity arose, the client became reluctant to reveal her feelings about what had occurred, when, and its specific impact on her life. The psychoanalytic approach would refer to this as resistance and the proper response would be to:

a. ignore the resistance in deference to the client's feelings.
b. mention the resistance, but make no effort to move the client forward on the matter.
c. confront the issue of resistance and make a point of addressing and exploring it with the client.
d. require the client to continue disclosing her feelings and coping with her pain as related to this highly sensitive matter.

141. A 52-year-old man has been referred to see a social worker for "family and work problems." Two months ago he lost his job as an executive in a major corporation, and has not found new work. On intake the social worker discovers his drinking has increased, and he reports feeling depressed most days. He can't seem to enjoy doing anything, not even golf, which he used to love. Rather, all he can seem to do is sleep and "sit around the house." He feels useless, empty, and helpless to change his situation. He has tried reading the want-ads, but he just can't seem to focus. He's gained over 18 lbs. He then adds, "Sometimes I seem to hear voices, telling me I'm just 'no good,' and that things will never get better. When that happens, I try to plug my ears, but it doesn't help. Only booze seems to get the voices to stop. Do you think I'm going crazy?" What is the client's probable primary diagnosis?

a. Major depressive disorder
b. Major depressive disorder with psychotic features
c. Alcohol use disorder
d. Alcohol-induced depressive disorder

142. A social worker begins to feel an unexpected affinity toward a client who reminds her of her father. This is a classic example of:

a. direct influence.
b. free association.
c. transference.
d. countertransference.

143. Key principles and concepts of the psychoanalytic approach include all of the following EXCEPT:

a. individuals are best understood through their social environment.
b. treatment is, by design, a short-term process, not to exceed six to twelve months.
c. behavior derives from unconscious motives and drives, and problematic experiences in the unconscious mind produce dysfunction and disorders.
d. resolution of problems is achieved by drawing out repressed information to produce greater understanding and behavioral change.

144. After identifying a specific behavior that a client wishes to change, the next priority for a social worker using a behavioral (behavior modification) approach is to:

a. identify and evaluate the antecedents and consequences of the behavior.
b. search for any related unconscious motivations or drives.
c. examine the emotions associated with the target behavior.
d. operationally define the behavior.

145. A hospital emergency room social worker is asked to see a client who was treated for traumatic assault injuries following a robbery. The client is clearly fearful, vulnerable, and overwhelmed. At the time of discharge the client expresses a reluctance to leave, voicing unrealistic fears of possible further assault. The most effective intervention approach in this situation would be which of the following?

a. Grief therapy
b. Crisis intervention
c. A psychoanalytic approach
d. A task-centered approach

146. A social worker is called to a hospital emergency room to see a 26-year-old university student. He came in claiming he was having a heart attack, but the medical work-up was entirely negative. He notes that at night his chest begins to tighten, his heart starts racing, his mouth goes dry, and his breathing becomes difficult. Next, his palms become sweaty and his hands start to tremble and tingle. Then he feels dizzy, nauseous, and worries that he's about to die. This is been going on for about six weeks. His studies have suffered, and he's becoming depressed and overwhelmed. He has no substance abuse history. Finally, he notes that his dad died of a heart attack at about his same age. His most likely diagnosis is:

a. panic disorder.
b. specific phobia.
c. acute stress disorder.
d. obsessive-compulsive disorder.

147. A social worker sees a newly married client who is having marital problems. The client discloses that her prior spouse was repeatedly unfaithful. She acknowledges a tendency to be overly suspicious and accusatory of her current spouse due to the persistent fears from her prior marriage. The social worker suggests that the client mentally construct a new or alternate scenario that applies to her new marriage in order to free herself from the old persistent fears. This approach would best be referred to as:

a. complementary therapy
b. collaborative therapy
c. narrative approach
d. social learning approach

148. The gender and typical age when the "Electra Complex" occurs is which of the following?

a. Females, 3-7 years of age
b. Males, 3-6 years of age
c. Females, 8-12 years of age
d. Males, 6-12 years of age

149. Strategic family therapy focuses on:

a. family communication.
b. family structure.
c. family rules and behavioral patterns.
d. family subsystems.

150. A group of individuals with one or more characteristics (social, physical, religious, or cultural) identified as being subordinately distinct in a larger societal context is referred to as a:

a. heterogeneous group.
b. minority group.
c. target group.
d. homogenous group.

Answers and Explanations

1. B: Executive functioning refers to higher order cognitive functioning. Specific examples include: organization (attention, decision-making, planning, sequencing, and problem solving), and regulation (initiation of action, self-control, and self-regulation). Lower order cognitive measures include: orientation to place, registration (recall of new learning immediately or within seconds, such as repeating words or numbers provided), recall (short-term and long-term memory), attention, and calculation.

2. D: A patient who is "oriented times four" is able to adequately identify: 1) himself (person); 2) his immediate location (place); 3) general features of time (day, month, year, etc.); and 4) his general circumstances (situation; i.e., in a counseling office seeking help, etc.).

3. D: The records should be retained as long as possible, preferably indefinitely. Records serve two purposes: 1) to maintain continuity between clinician-patient contacts; and 2) to document quality care. At a minimum, records must be kept in accordance with the state's statute of limitations. However, the social worker may not be legally protected even then, and certainly not after a patient's death (which could be construed, in some cases such as suicide, as a failure in quality care). Therefore, counseling records should be maintained as long as possible, and the longer the better.

4. C: In this situation the social worker should allow the patient to move into his motor home. The patient has a plan sufficient to meet his needs for food, clothing, and shelter. He has the legal right to choose where he wishes to live, even if others are not comfortable with his choice. Calling the police will not help, as they cannot force him to return to the facility. Adult protective services may have a subsequent role, if the patient begins to exhibit marked self-neglect or cognitive changes, but they cannot force the patient either. Finally, the patient is not eligible for an involuntary hold, as he is not placing himself or others in danger based upon a diagnosable mental illness, intoxication, or other substance abuse. Careful collateral planning, however, will be important (ensuring the daughter visits and checks in on him, etc.) to try and maximize his potential for success. After coping with the hardships of independent living, he may willingly return to assisted living.

5. C: Social workers are mandated to report even "suspicions" of child abuse. Therefore, the social worker should always call Child Protective Services and allow them to decide whether or not a formal investigation should be undertaken. It would be important, however, to also inform them of the nurse's prior experience, so that they may seek appropriate direction and avoid undue intervention that could otherwise damage an immigrant family's willingness to seek health care for a child in the future.

6. B: An evaluative test is reliable if it produces consistent results (i.e., if the same test was administered to the same subjects twice [i.e., "test-retest"], or to two similar groups with similar results [i.e., "split half"], it would produce similar results), and it is valid if it measures what is claims to measure. Consequently, a test may be reliable (consistently producing similar results in test-retest experiments) and yet invalid (failing to measure what it claims to measure. However, a truly valid test will always be reliable. Inter-rater reliability indicates whether the scoring process can be accurately carried out by different individuals using the same scoring procedure.

7. A: The best response is to tell the client to make an appointment to review his records. Although laws governing patient access to psychiatric records vary widely, most states do allow patients to view these records—although some limits are allowed in certain jurisdictions if the clinician has a

compelling concern regarding the welfare of the patient. Regardless, all states allow these records to be obtained by a patient's attorney under subpoena. While the clinician owns the psychiatric record, the information held within that record is generally viewed as belonging to the patient. Past research indicates that patients typically cope well with this information. Even so, some information may have a deleterious iatrogenic effect. At a minimum, the clinician should view the record in company with the patient, to explain, clarify, reassure, and otherwise guide the review process to a wholesome outcome. Become thoroughly informed of the laws in the area governing patient records access.

8. D: In most (but not all) states the social worker is a mandated reporter if Dependent Adult abuse is suspected. Where reporting laws exist, the social worker should call Adult Protective Services directly, and submit the necessary written report unless they indicate specifically that they do not wish to receive a duplicate report. While health care providers may occasionally offer help of this nature, it is not possible to discharge this mandated reporting requirement in this manner. Where no laws for Dependent Adult reporting exist, care should be taken not to violate confidentiality, and appropriate consultation should be obtained.

9. C: The onset of a substance abuse disorder typically occurs from late adolescence to early adulthood. An individual with a substance abuse disorder in adolescence is at risk for the disorder in adulthood as well.

10. C: The most appropriate diagnosis would be adjustment disorder with depressed mood. Criteria for this disorder includes a time-limited nature, usually beginning within three months of the stressful event, and lessening within six months—either with removal of the stressor or through new adaptation skills. Adjustment disorder is a "sub-threshold disorder," allowing for early classification of a temporary condition when the clinical picture remains vague. While the patient does have insomnia, it arises from the stressful loss and not as an independent condition. Many of the essential criteria for a major depression are absent (weight loss, psychomotor agitation, blunted affect, etc.), although without successful treatment this condition could emerge. The diagnosis of acute stress disorder is not appropriate as the precipitating event did not involve threatened or actual serious injury or death.

11. A: Psychotherapy is generally considered to be more long-term (and complex) in nature, and potentially depending more on a specific theoretical orientation, while counseling is often seen as shorter in duration and oriented more toward immediate problem-solving. However, these terms are often used interchangeably. The term "counseling" has been attributed to Frank Parsons, who used it in his writings in 1908. The renowned psychologist Carl Rogers adopted the term when the psychiatric profession refused to allow him to call himself a psychotherapist. Some in the psychoanalytic field still feel the term should be reserved to those providing formal psychoanalysis, but this is not a widely shared view.

12. D: Erickson's psychosocial development model focuses on conflicts at each stage of the lifespan and the virtue that results from finding balance in the conflict. The first 5 stages refer to infancy and childhood and the last 3 stages to adulthood:

- Intimacy vs. isolation (Young adulthood): Love/intimacy or lack of close relationships.
- Generativity vs. stagnation (Middle age): Caring and achievements or stagnation.
- Ego integrity vs. despair (Older adulthood): Acceptance and wisdom or failure to accept changes of aging/despair.

13. D: A cost-effective analysis measures the effectiveness of an intervention rather than the monetary savings. For example, annually 2 million nosocomial infections result in 90,000 deaths and an estimated $6.7 billion in additional health costs. From that perspective, decreasing infections should reduce costs, but there are human savings in suffering as well, and it can be difficult to place a dollar value on that. If each infection adds about 12 days to hospitalization, then a reduction of 5 infections (5 X 12 = 60) would result in a cost-effective savings of 60 fewer patient infection days.

14. D: Monoamine oxidase inhibitors (MAOIs), serotonin-norepinephrine reuptake inhibitors (SNRIs), and selective serotonin reuptake inhibitors (SSRIs) are three classes of medications that are used primarily to treat depressive disorders.

15. B: Initially, the identified client would be the husband. Upon entry of the wife into the picture, the identified client would be the couple, given that the social worker was working with them both and seeing them only jointly. After the passage of time, however, and upon identification of issues requiring primary work with the wife, the identified client would be the wife. Ideally, the social worker would have come to closure with the husband more formally, identifying specifically that the focus had shifted from them as a couple to a primary endeavor with the wife. Regardless, the information now being entered in the clinical record is exclusively that related to the wife, and the husband should no longer be privy to that content. In keeping with this, the identified client has become the wife.

16. A: Because of the high co-morbidity rate between substance abuse and other disorders, the social worker needs to look at any patterns of substance use by individuals who suffer from other disorders. Conversely, substance abuse may mask symptoms of other disorders.

17. D: Although it is ideal for social workers to receive specific training regarding each of the individual minority populations they typically serve, they should still ensure that someone from an unfamiliar background receives needed services even where no staff with special training in that background is available.

18. B: The Health Insurance Portability and Accountability Act (HIPAA) addresses the rights of the individual related to privacy of health information. Health care workers must not release any information or documentation about a patient's condition or treatment without consent. The individual has the right to determine who may be given access to information considered "protected health information" (PHI). This includes all "individually identifiable health information" such as health history, condition, treatments in any form, and any related documentation. Personal information can be shared with a spouse, legal guardians, and those with durable power of attorney only if: 1) the patient agrees (or at least does not object), or 2) when it is professionally determined to be in the patient's "best interest" for certain specific and essential information to be provided (i.e., "directly relevant to the involvement of a spouse, family members, friends, or other persons identified by a patient, in the patient's care or payment for health care").

19. D: The best course of action is to disclose limited information. Personal revelations are normally discouraged in a therapeutic relationship. They can turn the counseling experience into a mutual sharing process, robbing the client of proper attention. They can also cause the client to devalue the social worker if any revelation comes as an unwanted surprise. An exception to this rule exists when the therapeutic context is entirely centered in the information to be revealed—such as in a drug and alcohol rehabilitation program, where the sole purpose of the counseling is to address the issue being revealed (usually a group setting, where self-disclosure is essential to the process).

Disclosures must not occur early, before trust is in place, and the group leader should always clearly understand his or her full intent and goals before revealing any personal information.

20. B: People with borderline personality disorder exhibit variable moods and impulsive behavior along with a tendency to view others negatively. People with this disorder are very social yet have significant difficulty maintaining relationships.

21. A: Cultural competences is best defined as the ability to work well with diverse groups. Quality training, wide-ranging knowledge, and the ability to recognize stereotypes, prejudices, and biases are all important contributors to cultural competence; however, only when a social worker also possesses the capacity to properly apply this information, can he or she work well with diverse populations.

22. A: Root cause analysis (RCA) is a retrospective attempt to determine the cause of an event, such as a death or other sentinel event. RCA involves interviews, observations, and review of medical records. External benchmarking monitors data from outside an institution, such as national rates of infections, and compares them to internal data. Internal trending compares internal rates of one area or population with another. Tracer methodology looks at the continuum of care a patient receives from admission to post-discharge, using a selected patient's medical record as a guide.

23. D: The null hypothesis for this study would state that there shall be no measurable difference in depression symptom reporting between the control group and the intervention group. The null hypothesis (often designated as "H_0") proposes that no relationship exists between two variables (often designated "x" and "y") other than that arising from chance alone. If a study's results demonstrate no difference, then the null hypothesis is "accepted." If differences emerge, then the study "failed to reject the null hypothesis." Statistical testing does not prove any hypotheses, but instead disproves them via rejection.

24. C: Manic episodes are commonly seen in bipolar disorder and are characterized by such factors as a decreased need for sleep, racing thoughts and unrealistic ideation. Criteria for a manic episode in adults are that the episode lasts most of the day for at least one week.

25. B: A first manic episode experienced after age forty is highly unlikely with bipolar disorder and more likely would be due to a medical condition or, perhaps, a substance abuse issue. The average age for the first manic episode is the early 20's.

26. B: Prejudice is basing one's feelings, attitudes and beliefs regarding a specific group of people upon preconceived ideas, rumors and inferences. Although the other words are useful, they only describe certain qualities or behaviors arising from prejudice.

27. C: Clinical pathways should be based on evidence-based research, which refers to the use of current research and patient values in practice to establish an idealized plan of care. Research may be the result of large studies of best practices, or it may arise from individual research efforts using observations in practice about the effectiveness of a particular treatment. Evidence-based research requires a commitment to ongoing research and outcomes evaluation. Evidence-based research requires a thorough understanding of research methods, including internal and external validity.

28. C: A type I error refers to rejecting the null hypothesis when the null hypothesis is true. A failure to randomize research participants will potentially introduce bias, and may provide grounds upon which to invalidate a study, but it is not a type I error. Assuming a normal statistical distribution when it is skewed will violate the assumptions necessary to apply a proper statistical model to the analysis of data.

29. B: The family should be encouraged to stay and talk to the patient, as hearing is usually the last of the senses to fail. Typical physical changes associated with death include:

- Sensory: Reduced sensations of pain and touch. Decreased vision and hearing
- Cardiovascular: Tachycardia followed by bradycardia, dysrhythmia, and hypotension.
- Respiratory: Tachypnea, progressing to Cheyne-Stokes respiration.
- Muscular: Muscles relax, the jaw sags, and the ability to swallow and talk is lost.
- Urinary: Output decreases (accompanied by incontinence), and anuria follows.
- Integumentary: Skin becomes cold, clammy, cyanotic, and waxy. Skin in the coccygeal area often tears.

30. A: There is significant overlap between the symptoms of bipolar disorder and borderline personality disorder, and the social worker must take care to differentiate between the two. Borderline personality disorder is characterized by interpersonal issues, while bipolar disorder is more likely to have a biological etiology.

31. D: The causes of many cases of early-onset intellectual disability are difficult to determine. However, major categories of risk include genetic conditions, problems during pregnancy (including at and after birth), poverty and cultural deprivation.

32. A: A type II error refers to the failure to reject the null hypothesis when the null hypothesis is false. Invalid assumptions regarding raw data (i.e., skewed data that was assumed to follow a normal, or "bell shaped" distribution) can lead to the selection of a statistical analysis model that will produce inaccurate output. Rejecting the null hypothesis when the null hypothesis is true is a type I error. Making an error in mathematical calculations is one way to introduce error, but it is not a type II error. This is less common in the computer age, where most calculations have been automated.

33. D: Bipolar disorder is primarily a mood disorder, while schizophrenia is characterized more by disordered thought patterns.

34. B: Discrimination is basing the opportunities, options, and benefits available to a specific group of people based upon preconceptions and assumptions. Bigotry is an intolerance of other ideas and beliefs. Prejudice is accepting unconfirmed information that may be situationally or individually unique, and assuming them to be valid for an entire group or class people. Misogyny refers to a hatred or distrust of women.

35. D: Failure mode and effects analysis (FMEA) is a team-based prospective analysis method that attempts to identify and correct failures in a process before utilization to ensure positive outcomes. Steps include definition, team creation, description (flow chart), brainstorming, identification of potential causes of failures, listing potential adverse outcomes, assignment of a failure severity rating (1 is slight and 10 is death), assignment of a frequency/occurrence rating, assignment of a detection rating, calculation of a risk priority number, and the reduction of potential failures and identification of performance measures.

36. A: Team members usually observe the leader and determine who controls the meeting and how control is exercised, while beginning to form alliances. Arguing is counterproductive, and following strict rules of discourse may not solve power issues and may be too restrictive for small collaborative groups. Group interactions often become less formal as members develop rapport and are more willing to help and support each other to achieve goals. Rotating leadership roles can

lead to a lack of focus as styles may vary widely. The leader is responsible for organizing the group, clarifying methods to achieve work, and the means of working together toward a common goal.

37. B: The best response is to refuse to use the form. No client or client population is beneath the ethical standards of the field. An appropriate information release form stipulates a limited period of time beyond which the form expires, the specific kind of information to be released, the specific purpose for which the information is to be provided, and a specific individual or entity to whom/which the information will be provided. While obtaining an information release is indeed a "hassle" it is the ethical standard of care in the field, and deviation from it can open a practitioner to legal liability. The fact that a given client, or client population, may be unaware of this does not excuse the social worker from using an ethically appropriate form in keeping with expected standards of care. Any limitations to confidentiality—such as mandatory reporting if a client expresses intent to commit a crime or harm another—belong on a treatment consent form, rather than on an information release form.

38. B: The Mini-cog test assesses dementia by having patients remember and repeat 3 common objects and draw a clock face indicating a particular time. The MMSE assesses dementia through a series of tests, including remembering the names of 3 common objects, counting backward, naming, providing location, copying shapes, and following directions. The Digit Repetition Test assesses attention by asking the patient to repeat the 2 number, then 3, then 4 and so on. The Confusion Assessment Method is used to assess delirium, not dementia.

39. D: The four most common minority classifications are age, gender, race (ethnicity), sexual orientation.

40. B: This client is most likely experiencing a delusion. Delusions are inaccurate beliefs held by an individual. These delusional beliefs are overwhelmingly contraindicated by known reality.

41. C: Deinstitutionalization refers to changes in policy and law that led to the release of many mental health patients who would have otherwise remained in institutional settings. Involuntary hospital commitment (i.e., in an asylum) became increasingly common up to the 1950s. However, the Community Mental Health Act of 1963 began to reverse this trend, as did the 1999 US Supreme Court ruling in Olmstead vs. LC. In 1970 there were 413,066 beds in state and county mental hospitals, which fell to 119,033 by 1988, and to 63,526 by 1998. This era has since come to be called the era of "deinstitutionalization." Sometimes over done, issues of homelessness among the mentally ill, and "re-institutionalization" in the prison system have been noted.

42. B: Thought insertion/withdrawal is a type of delusion characterized by the belief that others are putting thoughts into or taking thoughts out of one's mind.

43. B: The Occupational Safety and Health Administration (OSHA) regulates workplace safety, including disposal methods for sharps, such as needles. OSHA requires that standard precautions be used at all times and that staff be trained to use precautions. OSHA requires procedures for post-exposure evaluation and treatment, and the availability of the hepatitis B vaccine for healthcare workers. OSHA regulates occupational exposure to infections, and establishes standards to prevent the spread of blood-borne pathogens, as well as regulating the fitting and use of respirators.

44. B: Alzheimer's disease causes atrophy of the brain tissue and is the most common form of dementia. Cognitive deficits are a common result of this disease.

45. C: Of successful suicides, 49% of those studied had a prior suicide attempt history. Of those previously seen by a mental health professional, 78% had denied having any suicidal ideation at their last contact.

46. C: The Braden scale is used to assess and predict the risk of a patient developing pressure sores. The Norton Scale is also used to predict pressure sores, and is based on scores in 5 categories (physical, mental, activity, mobility, and incontinence). The Pressure Ulcer Scale for Healing (PUSH) is used to assess improvement or deterioration of existing ulcers based on measurements, exudate, and tissue type. The Diabetic Foot Ulcer Scale assesses the quality of life of those with diabetic foot ulcers.

47. A: The primary purpose of interdisciplinary teams is the sharing of ideas and perspectives to solve problems. Collaboration requires open sharing and respect for the expertise of other professionals. Interdisciplinary teams may include doctors, nurses, and other members of the allied health professions as well. While cost-saving, timesaving, and improved patient satisfaction may (and often do) result from innovative approaches to problem solving, these are secondary benefits from effective interdisciplinary collaboration.

48. C: Ethnocentrism is the belief that one's personal background (i.e. race, culture, religion, etc.) is superior to that of others.

49. A: This patient is exhibiting dependence in response to stress. Typical psychological responses to stress include:

- Dependence: The patient has an inability to make decisions, requires constant reassurance, and calls nurses/families frequently.
- Depression: The patient is withdrawn and sad, fails to take treatments and/or misses appointments, and may be at risk for suicide.
- Anger: The patient is belligerent, uncooperative, and blames others.
- Confusion: The patient is forgetful, disoriented, and bewildered.
- Passivity: The patient defers to others, feeling he/she has no control.

50. D: CQI stands for "continuous quality improvement." This is an outgrowth of the quality assurance (QA) programs of the 1980s, and is intended to symbolize the fact that quality improvement is a never-ending process. Continuing education, problem resolution brainstorming, cause and effect "fishbone diagramming," process flowcharts, improvement storyboards, and implementation of the "plan, do, check, act" method of problem-solving and process improvement are all examples of CQI.

51. D: All staff members are responsible for identifying performance improvement projects. Performance improvement must be a continuous process. Continuous Quality Improvement (CQI) is a management philosophy that emphasizes the effectiveness of an organization and the systems and processes within that organization, rather than focusing on specific individuals. Total Quality Management (TQM) is a management philosophy that espouses a commitment to meeting the needs of the customers (patients and staff) at all levels within an organization. Both management philosophies recognize that change can be made in small steps and should involve staff at all levels.

52. A: The five most common classifications of race include Asian, Black, Hispanic, Native American, and White.

53. C: The paraphilia category of sexual disorders includes pedophilia, and it is the type of sexual disorder most likely to be brought to a social worker's attention.

54. C: Healthy People 2020 outlines leading health indicators and national objectives to improve health and reduce the risks of disease in order to improve life expectancy and quality of life. Leading health indicators include: 1) Access to health services. 2) Clinical preventive services. 3) Environmental quality. 4) Injury and violence. 5) Maternal, infant, and child health. 6) Mental health. 7) Nutrition, physical activity, and obesity. 8) Oral health. 9) Reproductive and sexual health. 10) Social determinants. 11) Substances abuse. 12) Tobacco. Additionally Healthy People 2020 includes many focus areas that relate to each of the 10 leading health indicators.

55. B: The steps of the Roberts crisis intervention model are as follows:

1. Assess lethality
2. Establish rapport
3. Identify problems
4. Deal with feelings
5. Explore alternatives
6. Develop an action plan
7. Follow-up

56. D: The Agency for Healthcare Research and Quality (AHRQ) of the US Department of Health and Human Services provides research and funding for the development of evidence-based practice guidelines. The AHRQ has sponsored the development of surveys for assessment of patient safety and is actively involved in outcomes research. The AHRQ research centers specialize in research related to patient safety, quality improvement, outcomes, assessment of clinical practices and technology, healthcare delivery systems, primary and preventive care, and heath care costs.

57. C: Frotteurism is a type of paraphilia, or sexual disorder, in which an individual gains sexual enjoyment by touching genitalia to a non-consenting or unsuspecting individual.

58. D: Some apparent mental health symptoms may arise from certain culture-specific dictates of behavior, mood, or thought processes. For example, talking with ghosts or other spirits, seeing hallucinations or visions, hearing voices, etc., can all be attributed to certain cultural and/or religious groups. In such situations, the individual should not receive a mental illness diagnosis.

59. C: Adult learners tend to be practical and goal-oriented, so they tend to remain organized and keep their educational goals in mind while learning. Other characteristics include:

- Self-directed: Adults prefer active involvement and responsibility.
- Knowledgeable: Adults can relate new material to information with which they are familiar by life experience or education.
- Relevancy-oriented: Adults like to know how they will use information.
- Motivated: Adults like to see evidence of their own achievement, such as gaining a certificate.

60. D: The Instrumental Activities of Daily Living (IADL) tool assesses financial ability (ability to pay bills, budget, and keep track of finances), telephone use, shopping, food preparation, housekeeping, laundry, transportation availability (ability to drive or use public transportation), and medications (ability to manage prescriptions and take medications). The Barthel Index of Activities of Daily Living assesses 10 categories, usually including bathing, toileting, ascending or descending stairs, feeding, mobility, personal grooming, urinary and fecal control, transferring, and ambulatory/wheelchair status.

61. D: Unlike major depressive disorder, which includes severe symptoms and lasts at least two weeks, dysthymic disorder has less intense symptoms and continues for two years or more.

62. B: Depression is the most common lifetime disorder. Some people may have one major episode, while others experience it as a recurring problem throughout their life.

63. B: A professional interpreter is the most appropriate option. Selecting a relative or friend risks violating client confidentiality, as does asking another staff person to become involved. Further, non-professional persons may not have an adequate grasp of special terminology needed to properly address medical, legal, or psychiatric concerns. Of note: written words are "translated," while spoken words are "interpreted."

64. B: The best time to initiate conflict resolution is when conflict first emerges, but before open conflict and hardening of positions. Resolution steps include:

1. Allowing both parties to present their side without bias.
2. Encouraging cooperation through negotiation and compromise.
3. Maintaining focus and avoiding arguments.
4. Evaluating the need for renegotiation, a formal resolution process, or a 3rd party mediator.
5. Utilizing humor and empathy to diffuse tension.
6. Summarizing and outlining key arguments.

65. C: Maslow stated that human behavior is motivated by various needs, and posited that there is a hierarchy of need beginning with basic needs and progressing to personal needs. Maslow theorized that working toward self-actualization is a lifelong process that may involve progress in multiple directions rather than in one direction. Failure results in depression and diminished feelings of value:

- 1st Level (the base): Physiological needs.
- 2nd Level: Safety and security.
- 3rd Level: Love/Belonging.
- 4th Level: Self-esteem.
- 5th level (the apex): Self-actualization.

66. D: Goal congruence, which, according to Drisko (2009), is the fourth of five key factors required for a quality therapeutic relationship between client and clinician. The five key factors are as follows:

- Affective attunement
- Mutual affirmation
- Joint efforts to resolve missteps
- Goal congruence
- Using varying types of empathy

67. C: There is no requirement that information be disclosed to an employer providing coverage, unless the employee has previously stipulated information to be released in consenting to coverage and services. Payment for coverage by an employer does not, in and of itself, entitle the employer to any private client information. Even under conditions of subpoena, social workers may be able to limit the scope of information shared, or even claim "privileged communication" status in response to orders to testify.

68. C: The appropriate steps are as follows: Establish a rapport, summarize legal and ethical obligations, complete a service contract, and assess the client. Establishing a rapport usually includes a review of the client's presenting problem, though it also includes fostering trust, showing empathy and concern, and demonstrating a willingness to be non-judgmental about the presenting issue. Summarizing legal and ethical obligations includes addressing mandatory reporting issues and client confidentiality. A service contract covers mutual roles and expectations, major goals, the anticipated course of treatment, and how to handle issues of non-performance. Assessment should cover the client's personal mental health history, medical history (including substance abuse), family history, work history, and social history. It may also include an evaluation of the client's mood, safety, intellectual functioning, and emotional stability.

69. A: The life course theory of aging is a sociological model that views aging as a lifelong process of social, psychological, and biological changes. The process of change begins in infancy and continues through older adulthood, and is viewed within cultural, economic, social, and historic contexts. Key concepts include:

- The social and historical contexts and environmental location.
- Individual, generational, and historical time.
- Degrees of heterogeneity or variability.
- Social connections.
- Personal agency and control, and control cycles.
- The past as related to future.

70. C: Bureaucracy refers to an organization that is arranged hierarchically, with numerous departments and units through which segments of specialized services are provided, moving toward achievement of a common goal.

71. D: The unconscious mind is involved in this behavior, according to Freud. Freud addresses three areas of cognition: 1) the conscious mind, of which individuals are fully aware; 2) the preconscious mind, involving thoughts and feelings of which individuals may be immediately unaware but which can be accessed easily if desired; and 3) the unconscious mind, containing thoughts and feelings of which all individuals remain entirely unaware. The goal of Psychoanalytic Theory is to address this aspect of the mind and its role and influence on the conscious and preconscious mind, along with the resultant thoughts, emotions, and behaviors.

72. A: Striving for patient satisfaction is a long-term outcome. Process is important, but both short-term and long-term outcome measures should be established based upon clinical efficacy, rather than patient satisfaction (e.g., patients may not always appreciate essential treatments and interventions). Short-term outcomes show results directly related to process and allow modification of the process, but long-term outcomes (such as patient satisfaction) often relate to general quality of care and may be used retrospectively to evaluate the process or plan for future care. Three types of outcome measures should be identified: clinical, patient functioning, and patient satisfaction.

73. D: A social assessment report focuses on a client's social and relational functioning. This form of client assessment may also be called a "social history."

74. D: Several factors can cause a person to be at a higher risk of attempting suicide, including having had thoughts about suicide in the past, a history of the behavior in one's family and a history of high mobility.

75. B: A structured questionnaire or checklist can be particularly helpful if a client is having difficulty exploring, formulating, or discussing his situation or concerns. The document provides information that prompts the client, and thereby aids in opening up the problem and specific concerns. Questionnaires and checklists can also be particularly helpful if the situation being evaluated is complex or risk laden and the social worker needs to be particularly thorough (e.g., a suicide assessment, etc.).

76. A: The interpreter should have training in medical vocabulary for both languages. Just speaking the languages well does not mean that the translator will adequately interpret specialized vocabulary. It is not necessary for the interpreter to know the patient's history, as the interpreter's job is only to interpret what is said, not add to it or augment it based on prior knowledge. While onsite interpreters are ideal, interpretation can be provided through a speakerphone at a distance.

77. C: Cathexis refers to the attachment (whether conscious or unconscious), of mental or emotional ("psychosexual") energy (i.e., feelings and significance) to an idea, object, image, or, most commonly, a person. Psychically, pain arises from loss. Cathexes are "objective" when they are directed at the external world, and "narcissistic" when they have meaning only for the subject. Significant pain imposes a substantial narcissistic cathexis that tends to "empty the ego." The result of prolonged pain is often "regression," as the ego becomes less able to serve its "anti-cathexis" role of imposing rationality and executive functioning on a situation characterized by severe pain (whether physical or emotional).

78. A: Frontline organizational services are not one of the basic functions of administrators. Services "in the trenches" are provided by employee staff, instead. Administrative functions do include advocacy, conflict resolution/mediation, and planning/delegation.

79. A: An eco-map (also called an "ecological map" or an ecogram, especially if it includes a genogram) helps individuals and families visually depict the quality of relationships with others, within the community and with important resources in their lives. While a genogram is limited to "family tree" depictions, the eco-map is broadly constructed to include multiple other important relationships to people, systems, communities, extended family, resources, services, etc. It can explore a range of things, from relationships to finances. Lines connecting the "client" (an individual or a family, at the center of the diagram) have direction arrows to depict influence flow (which may be bidirectional), strength of the relationship, and quality of the relationship (i.e., dominant, powerful, and angry would be depicted by the direction of the power, a thick line would indicate a strong connection, and the line would be drawn wavy or red if the relationship is stressful).

80. B: The client is describing the features of avoidant personality disorder. Criteria includes being worried about social situations, unwillingness to try new activities, avoiding activities once found enjoyable if they are social.

81. D: There is no Cluster D – only A, B, and C. These cluster descriptions have been provided by authors in various academic sources, although they only loosely describe each cluster's content. Cluster A includes: paranoid, schizoid, and schizotypal personality disorders. Cluster B includes: antisocial, borderline, histrionic, and narcissistic personality disorders. Finally Cluster C includes: obsessive/compulsive, avoidant, and dependent personality disorders. Clusters tend to run in families.

82. B: This accommodation is an example of alloplastic behavior. This is a form of adaptation in which an individual changes aspects of his environment in order to better accommodate competing

needs or demands. Changes in oneself or one's behavior (as opposed to the environment), in order to better accommodate competing needs or demands is called "autoplastic behavior."

83. B: Reacting and responding to facts instead of feelings to avoid confrontations and diffuse anger helps facilitate communications with intra- and interdisciplinary teams. Professional communication skills to facilitate team communication also include:

- Avoiding interpreting others statements, interrupting, giving unsolicited advice, or jumping to conclusions -- all of which may interfere with the free flow of ideas.
- Listening actively and asking questions for clarification rather than challenging other people's ideas.
- Clarifying information or opinions to help avoid misunderstandings.
- Communicating openly and respecting others' opinions.

84. D: The Wechsler Adult Intelligence Scale (WAIS) was introduced in 1955 as a revised update of the Wechsler-Bellevue Intelligence Scale of 1939. Perhaps the next most common scale used is the Stanford-Binet Intelligence Scale, first released in 1916, which was derived from the French Binet-Simon Intelligence Scale of 1905. The median score for the WAIS is 100, with a standard deviation of 15 (i.e., scores between 85 and 115), which encompasses about 68% of all adults. It is administered to individuals over the age of 16. Individuals between the ages of 6-16 may be given the Wechsler Intelligence Scale for Children (WISC).

85. B: Interdepartmental funding allocation is something done at the administrative level, rather than by supervisory staff. A supervisor's role involves being a role model, recruitment and orientation, day-to-day management, staff training/education/development, staff assessments and reviews, advocating for staff and program needs, evaluating the program for ongoing improvement, and providing support and counsel to staff.

86. C: V Codes are problems or conditions not due to a mental disorder, but that require clinical attention (e.g., noncompliance with treatment or parent-child relational problem). Most of these codes, borrowed from the International Classification of Disease (ICD) manual provide for severity and treatment course specifiers such as mild, moderate, and severe, as well as by prior history, in partial remission, or full remission. Where a specific diagnosis is expected, but has not been finalized, a code may be qualified as a provisional diagnosis. A diagnosis should also be accompanied by a diagnostic differential or formulation, in which the criteria in support of the diagnosis (and against other options) are summarized.

87. A: This should occur at or around 24 months. Margaret Mahler's three stages of development are: 1) the autistic stage; 2) the symbiotic stage; and 3) the separation-individuation stage. The separation-individuation stage consists of four sub-stages, the third of which (the rapprochement substage) is completed sometime between 14-24 months of age. Then, the infant enters the last substage (the "object constancy substage"), which is completed by the infant sometime after 24 months of age.

88. C: Reciprocal evaluation is not a program evaluation method. Outcome evaluation focuses on end-results after the program is completed. Participatory evaluation is an inductive, community-centered evaluative approach. Process-oriented evaluation (also called "formative evaluation") analyzes a certain point in time under specifically selected conditions (e.g., at planning or implementation point, etc.) in order to determine if the segment being evaluated is functioning properly, which allows both strengths and weaknesses to be identified.

89. C: Pervasive developmental disorders is NOT a DSM-5 category. The DSM-5 classifications are:

- Neurodevelopmental disorders:
- Schizophrenia spectrum and other psychotic disorders
- Bipolar and related disorders
- Depressive disorders
- Anxiety disorders
- Obsessive-compulsive and related disorders
- Trauma- and stressor-related disorders
- Dissociative disorders
- Somatic symptom and related disorders
- Feeding and eating disorders
- Elimination disorders
- Sleep-wake disorders
- Sexual dysfunctions
- Gender dysphoria
- Disruptive, impulse-control, and conduct disorders
- Substance-related and addictive disorders
- Neurocognitive disorders
- Personality disorders
- Paraphilic disorders
- Other mental disorders
- Medication-induced movement disorders
- Other conditions that may be a focus of clinical attention

Most disorders that were classified as pervasive developmental disorders under the DSM-IV will now fall under the classification neurodevelopmental disorders and more specifically communication disorders or autism spectrum disorder.

90. B: The decision regarding the issue(s) that should be addressed first should be made by the client, in exploration with the social worker. The client's right of self-determination must control the treatment process (except in situations of specific court-ordered treatment). While the social worker may suggest priorities, the broad goals and specific objectives of the treatment plan must be decided by the client, even if the social worker does not entirely agree. During the course of treatment, revisions to the focus and/or process of treatment (i.e., the treatment plan's goals and objectives) may become necessary and proper, but any such changes must ultimately be decided by the client and not imposed by the social worker.

91. A: The "aggregate evaluation" approach is not a method of program "outcome evaluation." The "decision-oriented" approach utilizes agency data, surveys, interviews, and observations to identify which elements in a program are functioning well and which need improvement. The "experimental evaluation" approach is a very formal endeavor, wherein requisite independent variables and a dependent variable are defined and then testing is undertaken to examine causality. The "performance audits" approach uses an independent, third-party evaluator to examine program performance standards and outcomes.

92. D: Transmuting internalization is the process through which a cohesive self is achieved by incorporating the perceptions and functions of healthy significant others and objects into internalized self structure. Empathic mirroring is the process by which the mother demonstrates ("reflects") care and understanding of the child, in turn helping the child to develop a self-identity.

Rapprochement is a term from object relations theory, indicating the need for an infant to seek independence while still retaining security. Differentiation is a substage in object relations theory, where an infant begins to look at the outside world, as opposed to the inward focus common to infants younger than five months of age.

93. D: First the social worker should explore and discuss the client's feelings about termination. It may be possible to ameliorate the client's distress by exploring the feelings related to termination. This may well involve assuring the client that he or she can always return for further contact at any time, or even schedule a follow-up appointment in the near future. Revising the termination plan should not occur unless other reasonable options have been explored and attempted. Where early discussion about termination is incorporated in the initial treatment plan, and where accomplishment of client goals is tracked, noted, and discussed, healthy accommodation to termination is enhanced.

94. C: This client/ social worker interaction could be improved in several ways. The first comment is shallow and does not address the feelings presented. The second comment would have better included a more descriptive word, such as "frustrated" or "furious." The final statement gives inappropriate reassurance of what will happen in the course of therapy, which the social worker has no right to ensure.

95. D: Peer reviews are not a form of participatory evaluation. Cluster evaluations are used to examine several program facets at one time. Based on pluralism, they allow multiple programs to determine how to solve joint problems. Action research is an informal method of review conducted by individuals directly affected by the issue being examined. Self evaluations are a method by which involved staff members evaluate a program.

96. C: Early remission is no stimulant use criteria being met (except for craving) for at least 3 but less than 12 months. Sustained remission is no stimulant use criteria being met (except for cravings) for 12 months or longer. The terms full and partial are no longer used to describe remission.

97. B: Consultants do not have "administrative authority," but function only in an advisory capacity.

98. B: The primary focus of Gestalt psychology is on the "here and now." Gestalt psychology seeks to unify and integrate the personality, and to create "wholeness." It sees individuals as empowered agents able to control and regulate their future by personal choice. A focus on the past and its influence on the present and future is minimized (as compared with psychoanalytic theory).

99. B: The most likely diagnosis would be mild neurocognitive disorder due to traumatic brain injury. A diagnosis of intellectual disability requires both cognitive impairment (an IQ of 70 or lower) and an onset before the age of 18. The condition would be identified as a neurocognitive disorder due to traumatic brain injury, given the history. Dementia is no longer used as a DSM-5 diagnosis- it has been subsumed under neurocognitive disorder.

100. D: Termination can be undertaken for many reasons: 1) when mutually agreed upon goals have been met; 2) when a client must move; 3) following client- social worker conflicts; 4) upon referral to a specialist; and 5) because of finance/insurance changes. Efforts should be made for this to be a positive experience.

101. C: Narrative recording consolidates and reports all information (including progress, interventions, and conclusions) in an ongoing story form.

102. A: The most appropriate diagnosis would be oppositional defiant disorder. The degree of discord is substantial, and the level of verbal conflict is high, thus oppositional defiant disorder would be the most appropriate diagnosis. A parent-child relational problem tends to be less severe in nature, while conduct disorder is much more severe (i.e., involves violations of the rights of others, physical aggression, or property damage, persistent truancy, etc.). Intermittent explosive disorder addresses impulsive acts of aggression or violence (as opposed to premeditated or planned behaviors). Persistent conduct disorder carried into adulthood may meet criteria for antisocial personality disorder.

103. A: Individuals over the age of 50 are moving into the stage of ego integrity versus despair. This is the last developmental stage of life where one reconciles his or her relationships with others, and comes to accept his or her life achievements (including where dreams were not met). Individuals unable to secure relationship and ego integrity will experience a sense of despair. Intimacy versus isolation is the young adult stage, characterized by building multiple important relationships. Identity versus role confusion is the adolescent stage, where one forges a sense of self and his or her place in society. Generativity versus stagnation is the mid-life stage, most characterized by learning to care about and nurture others, as opposed to a narcissistic preoccupation with oneself. Erikson was the first theorist to address human development across the entire lifespan.

104. D: Process recording is the type of record-keeping that chronologically and systematically records client information. Fact sheet information is obtained at the time of client intake, and subsequent entries are made after telephone conversations, face-to-face contacts, etc. This method of record-keeping is time consuming, but it provides a particularly complete summary of interactions, goals, and current issues.

105. D: This child should be considered to have mild intellectual disability. The term mental retardation has been replaced with intellectual disability after the federal statute named Rosa's law. While criteria for intellectual disability include having a deficit in intellectual capacity, which can be determined by IQ, the degree of severity is determined by adaptive functioning. The client being able to live alone while only needing support for specific activities indicates a severity level of mild.

106. C: The key feature to delirium is a rapid onset and fluctuating course throughout the day. Dementia has been encompassed by the term neurocognitive disorder which is characterized by a slow and persistent escalation of symptoms over an extended period of time. Diagnostically, the term senile is only an indicator of age (pre-senile refers to an onset prior to age 65; senile refers to an onset at age 65 or older). While overmedication is a possibility, there was not information provided to suggest this diagnosis, and thus the most likely diagnosis would be delirium due to a rapid onset medical condition (fever, bladder infection, early pneumonia, etc.) in an elderly individual.

107. A: Person-oriented recording focuses on goals, and is segmented into four sections:

- Factual information (a face sheet or database section)
- The assessment and expected treatment plan
- The progress notes
- The progress review entries (usually at 6-12 week intervals)

108. C: The pre-operational and concrete operational stages encompass these increasing elaborate understanding of death from ages 2-5 and 5-9. The sensorimotor stage encompasses birth to two years of age, and children in this stage have only a "here and not here" understanding of loss, at most. The formal operational stage extends from age 11 to age 15, and a child in this stage is

capable of hypothetical thinking, and is thus readily able to understand the essential aspects death and many of its more philosophical and existential concepts, as well.

109. C: The most appropriate diagnosis for the wife, given the relevant details, would be stimulant use disorder. The DSM-5 no longer separates substances abuse and dependence but now places all disorders under substance use disorder, substance intoxication, and substance withdrawal. Stimulant use disorder involves the need for escalating amounts of a substance to achieve intoxication, withdrawal symptoms, compulsive use in spite of a desire to stop, compromised social, occupational/educational, familial, and/or other important role compromise due to the use of an intoxicating substance, and includes severe physiological or compulsive use features. Severity is decided by the number of symptoms, and can be classified as mild, moderate, or severe.

110. A: The most appropriate diagnosis for this youth is Oppositional Defiant Disorder. Intermittent explosive disorder is only appropriate when a behavior is compulsive in nature. While anger may be a part of that picture, it tends to be an overreaction to a provocation; other relevant compulsions include gambling, skin-picking, kleptomania, etc. The hallmark of Conduct Disorder is deliberate cruelty, and wanton disregard for others rights and property. This client lacks any pervasive and long-standing evidence in this regard. Antisocial personality disorder is only diagnosed after the age of 18 when there was a history of conduct disorder prior to the age of 15.

111. B: Problem-oriented recording focuses largely on a client's ongoing issues and contains four components:

- Factual information
- A checklist section providing a rank-order roster of client issues
- A resolution plan
- Progress notes summarizing actions taken and results achieved

112. D: Alfred Adler's Adlerian theory also includes a biological view, largely absent in Psychoanalytic Theory, recognizing that hormonal changes, physical illness, chemical imbalances, and neurological disorders can dramatically influence capacity and behavior. It is important to note, however, that Alder still locates false beliefs, irrational thoughts, and misconceptions in the unconscious mind.

113. A: Typical symptoms of schizophrenia include: grossly disorganized or catatonic behavior and/or speech, delusions and/or hallucinations, blunted affect (poor or inappropriate expressive responses to external stimuli), autism (intense self-preoccupation). Continuous signs of symptoms must be present (allowing for waxing and waning fluctuations) for six or more months. There are five types: 1) paranoid; 2) disorganized; 3) catatonic; 4) undifferentiated; and, 5) residual. Early mild symptoms are sometimes referred to as prodromal schizophrenia. Common medications for treatment: Clozaril (clozapine), Haldol (haloperidol), Loxitane (loxapine), Mellaril (thioridazine), Prolixin (fluphenazine), Risperdal (risperidone), Stelazine (trifluoperazine), Thorazine (chlorpromazine), and Zyprexa (olanzapine).

114. C: The two major classifications of research are uantitative and qualitative. Quantitative research consists of objective experiments, surveys, and other examinations that use representative numerical data in descriptive or inferential analyses—used primarily to test theories. Qualitative research consists of subjective observations and interviews using systematic inductive processes to describe and define specific groups, individuals, or processes (for example, a "field study")—used primarily to develop theories.

115. A: Encopresis is the voluntary or involuntary passage of stool in an inappropriate place by a child over the age of four (i.e., past toilet training). This is a frequently misused term. It is most frequently applied to children and developmentally delayed adults. Adults with psychosis may warrant use of the term, although the term "fecal incontinence" is more commonly used for adults. A British literature review found only one use of the term in an adult that was not either psychotic or intellectually disabled—a 1932 case of a 36-year-old diagnosed with "infantile neurosis." The most typical etiology is stool impaction (constipation) compromising sphincter control and allowing leakage into the underclothing. However, emotional disorders, anxiety, or oppositional defiant disorder can sometimes underlie the behavior. Incidence of the condition drops steadily after age six.

116. D: Standard precautions were designed by the Occupational Safety and Health Administration to protect patients and employees of health care facilities (or anyone) who come in contact with bodily fluids (e.g., blood, saliva, vomit, feces). They mandate that protective barriers are used (e.g., gloves, eye coverings, gowns, aprons, masks); proper hand washing is performed before and after handling a patient, using soap and water, but also alcohol-based hand sanitizer; and the proper disposal of needles and other items that come in contact with patients in designated containers.

117. D: Statistical studies are not a separate form or category of study design. Statistics can be used in virtually any form of study, and thus it cannot be defined as a category of its own. Descriptive studies build upon known information in an attempt to further extend understandings and to provide new qualitative facts for further theorization. These studies require moderate rigor and control. Experimental studies use dependent variables (the variables of interest) and the manipulation of various independent variables to evaluate the resulting effects on the dependent variables. They require controlled conditions and the reduction or elimination of extraneous and intervening variables. These kinds of studies require the highest rigor and control. Exploratory studies are used in areas and subjects where little or nothing on the topic is known, or to expand existing knowledge. These studies require low levels of rigor and control, allowing for maximum flexibility in the exploration process.

118. B: Founded by Albert Ellis, rational emotive therapy utilizes the "ABC Theory of Emotion." It states that an event ("A"), elicits thoughts and beliefs ("B"), which directly result in specific behavioral consequences ("C"). Therefore, analyzing one's relevant thoughts and beliefs, and restructuring those that are dysfunctional or disturbed, will lead to increasingly healthy and functional responses.

119. B: Eco-systems theory (also known as life model theory) postulates that all individuals experience adaptation by which they attempt to achieve a "goodness of fit" to their physical and social environment. Thus, this blended family adapted by revising roles, rearranging the home as needed, and altering schedules and activities to accommodate each other.

120. B: Delirium is more frequently present in dementia patients than in patients without dementia. This is because patients with dementia are more tenuously balanced cognitively than those without dementia, and thus they succumb more readily to the condition. In elderly dementia patients, a low-grade fever or bladder infection may be sufficient for them to lapse into delirium. Because health care providers often do not know the patient's baseline level of cognition, dementia frequently masks delirium. Indeed, a diagnosis of delirium is missed more than 50% of the time. Rapid global deterioration in cognition (often, in hours to days) is the hallmark. Fever, electrolyte imbalances (usually due to dehydration), and medication toxicity are precipitating factors. A medical exam is therefore necessary for a proper diagnosis to be made.

121. B: The research process includes problem identification, background information, hypothesis formulation, operationalization, evaluation, and further theorization.

122. B: The most likely diagnosis is panic disorder. Criteria for generalized anxiety disorder specifies excessive worry about a number of events or activities as opposed to an isolated fear or concern. Further, it tends to persist for long periods rather than having an abrupt onset. Somatization disorder is characterized by complaints regarding several organ systems involving different body sites and functions, rather a single body organ. Post-traumatic stress disorder requires confronting an event or events that involve actual or threatened death or serious injury. The client was away at school, did not witness his father's death, and it didn't pose any direct threat to him. Panic attacks involve sudden onset, profound fear of death, and other symptoms such as those the client has described. Common treatment medications: Paxil, Klonopin, Tofranil, Celexa, Librium, Valium, Xanax.

123. A: This client is on the Conventional Level, Stage 3. The Theory of Moral Development was created by Lawrence Kohlberg, to extend and enhance Jean Piaget's theory. Overall, Kohlberg felt that the process of moral development was more complex and extended than that put forth by Piaget.

124. A: Single system designs are common to use by practitioners to evaluate their practice. The evaluation process involves: 1) problem identification (called the "target" of the research); 2) operationalization (selecting indices that represent the problem that can be measured; 3) determining the "phase" (the time over which measurement will occur), including a "baseline phase" (without intervention) and an "intervention phase." This may also include a "time series design," where data is collected at discrete intervals over the course of the study.

125. A: In early remission the criteria for a substance use disorder have previously been met, but none of those criteria are fulfilled (except for the criteria for craving) for at least three months but not more than 1 year. In sustained remission, none of those criteria are fulfilled (except for the criteria for craving) for 1 year or longer. If the client is in remission in a controlled environment, this should be specified. Some clients may be on maintenance therapy which is a replacement medication that can be taken to avoid withdrawal symptoms. The client could still be considered in remission from a substance use disorder if while using maintanance therapy, they do no meet any criteria for that substance use disorder except for craving. This client does not live in a controlled environment, such as a sober house, and can be considered in remission despite being in maintenance therapy as long as he has not met criteria for use disorder except craving.

126. A: Although lithium carbonate has been used for many years in the treatment of bipolar disorder, it is by no means the only medication used to treat the condition. In more recent years bipolar disorder has been treated with: 1) anticonvulsants (i.e., certain anti-seizure medications); 2) antidepressants, such as selective serotonin reuptake inhibitors (SSRIs), monoamine oxidase inhibitors (MAOIs), and, less commonly, tricyclic antidepressants; 3) antipsychotics, such as Haldol and Zyprexa; 4) calcium channel blockers (including blood pressure medications such as Nifedipine and Verapamil); and 5) Benzodiazepines, such as Xanax and Valium. Even electroconvulsive therapy has been successfully utilized.

127. D: Positive reinforcement, negative reinforcement, punishment, and extinction are the four kinds of reinforcement used in the Operant Conditioning Theory. Positive reinforcement (the most powerful of all) is the ADDITION of something pleasurable following a desirable behavior. Negative reinforcement involves taking something away to support the behavior (i.e., taking a break from an unpleasant task). Punishment involves adding something burdensome when an undesirable

behavior occurs. Extinction is the gradual withdrawal of a reinforcement until the target behavior has been fully modified (i.e., reducing the break period from a difficult task if the classroom gets noisy).

128. D: Time series only (Design A-B) is not one of the three. Design A consists of observation only, without any intervention. Design B is an intervention only, without any baseline measurement. Design B-C refers to an initial intervention with data recorded (B), followed by a revised intervention and renewed data recording (C).

129. D: Blunted affect is not a necessary element to diagnose schizophrenia. While a client with schizophrenia may present with a blunted affect, it is not necessary to make a diagnosis of schizophrenia. According to the DSM-5, criteria A of diagnosing schizophrenia includes that the client must present with 2 out the 3 following symptoms: delusions, hallucinations, or disorganized speech.

130. C: The most likely diagnosis is social anxiety disorder. The typical symptoms of panic disorder (dizziness, shortness of breath, palpitations, profuse sweating, tingling, hyperventilation, etc.) are absent. General anxiety disorder is focused more on excessive worry and stress about a variety of issues, and it persists in spite of any specific location or activity. Social phobia involves fears about being in social situations involving performance and scrutiny. While bodily function fears lend to a diagnosis involving agoraphobia, the site-specific nature of this situation validates the greater likelihood of a social phobia.

131. A: The four steps, in order, are attention, retention, reproduction, motivation. Bandura and his colleagues demonstrated that consequences (reinforcement, punishment, etc.) were not always necessary for behavioral change or other learning to take place. Simply observing someone else's activity could be sufficient. The four step pattern was as follows:

> 1. Attention -- the individual notices something in the environment. 2. Retention – he remembers what was noticed. 3. Reproduction – he copies what was noticed. 4. Motivation – the environment delivers a consequence (reinforcement or punishment), that affects the probability that the behavior will be repeated. Most advertising uses these principles: a product is presented as socially desirable (attention). The ad is remembered (retained), the purchase is made (reproducing the ad's direction to buy), and if social approval is forthcoming then further purchases will be made.

132. C: This is the "basic" single system design. This fundamental single system design is more complex than single system case study designs, as it includes a planned intervention and formal evaluation. Although it is flexible, easily operationalized, and easily produces clear evidence of change, etc., the primary drawback of this design is that it cannot demonstrate causation.

133. B: Malingering (though it is a V code (other conditions that may be a focus of clinical attention, it is not a diagnosis). Malingering involves feigning symptoms primarily to derive an <u>external reward</u> (lawsuit settlement, disability benefits, etc.). Illness anxiety disorder involves a misapprehension or misinterpretation of bodily symptoms. Factitious disorder involves a feigning of symptoms primarily in order to receive the attention offered when one assumes a sick role, even in the absence of external reward. Somatic symptom disorder is characterized by complaints regarding several organ systems involving different body sites and functions rather than a single body organ or situation.

134. C: The most likely diagnosis is borderline personality disorder. The key features of BPD involved instability in relationships and affect, poor self-image, and high impulsivity. Violations of

personal rights and apathy common to antisocial personality disorder are insufficiently pronounced. While evidence of histrionic behavior exists, the devaluation/over-valuation pattern common to BPD is not accounted for via histrionic personality disorder. Nor is the need for admiration, pervasive with narcissism, not otherwise addressed.

135. C: A reaction formation is a defense mechanism in which unacceptable emotions and impulses are controlled (or by which control is at least attempted) by exaggeration of the directly opposing tendency. Another example would be treating someone you very much dislike in an overly friendly manner. Or a woman professes profound hatred for a man who left her in order to cope with the pain he caused when he dismissed her deep love for him. In this way, one attempts to both hide and cope with their true feelings.

136. C: The model most commonly used by other social workers should not dictate framework selection. Various factors may constrain the practice framework chosen, but it should never be a matter of "popularity" alone. It may become necessary to utilize more than one framework, based upon a clientele's needs, the course of treatment, demands of an agency or an insurer. Regardless, when utilizing a practice framework, it should guide the social worker's approach with the client, and the treatment process.

137. B: The "additive" category is not a category of measurement. The ordinal category is used when a hierarchical arrangement exists, but the distance between each position is not necessarily equal (e.g., first, second, third runners in a race). The interval category can only be used when both a hierarchical and an equal-distant relationship between positions exists (e.g., a 1-10 scale). The ratio category is an interval scale with an absolute zero (a score of five is exactly one-half of ten, etc.).

138. D: Behavioral and cognitive approaches are practice approaches based on theoretical orientations, not frameworks. The ethnic-sensitive framework requires the social worker to view and engage issues from an ethnic and cultural perspective, and the feminist framework orients engagement from the perspective of gender and feminism. The systems framework focuses on behavioral issues as related to biological and social systems. The eco-system framework views behavior from an environmental adaptation perspective. The strengths framework focuses on issues from the vantage point of a client's strengths and the capacity to achieve goals. Finally, the generalist framework provides for an eclectic approach, utilizing a variety of frameworks and approaches as necessary.

139. D: The most likely diagnosis is borderline personality disorder. Individuals with this diagnosis will exhibit: frantic efforts to avoid real or imagined abandonment; unstable and intense interpersonal relationships (especially extremes of idealization and devaluation); an unstable sense of self; extreme impulsivity (e.g., spending, sex, drug use, reckless driving, binge eating, etc.); recurring suicidal behavior (gestures or threats, or self-mutilating behavior); affective instability due to reactivity of mood; chronic feelings of emptiness; intense anger (e.g., frequent displays of temper, recurrent physical fights); transient, stress-related paranoid ideation; or severe dissociative symptoms.

140. C: Confronting the issue of resistance and making a point of addressing and exploring it with the client is the proper response. The psychoanalytic (or psychodynamic) approach provides for direct confrontational address in situations of resistance. Drawing from psychoanalytic theory, ego psychology theory, object relations theory, and psychosocial theory, this theoretical orientation sees resistance as a way to avoid bringing up repressed memories, and unconscious/subconscious information necessary to growth, understanding, and overcoming.

141. B: The probable primary diagnosis is major depressive disorder with psychotic features. The precipitating event was his job loss, which led to depression. When the depression deepened he started "hearing voices," and he drank to cope with the negative messages (and to cope with his depression). Therefore, while the alcohol use must be included in his diagnostic formulation, it would not be his primary diagnosis. Of note, the diagnosis of major depression with psychotic features is missed about 25% of the time in an emergency room, with only the depression typically identified.

142. D: Countertransference refers to the unconscious feelings, desires, defenses, and reactions to a client. Transference refers to the unconscious feelings and reactions of the client toward the social worker. Free association is a technique wherein the client is directed to express any thought that comes to mind to explore unconscious mind and desires. Direct influence refers to suggestions and advice given a client to enhance understanding and behavioral change.

143. B: The psychoanalytic approach is generally a long-term therapeutic orientation, as time is required to identify, expose, and resolve repressed and unconscious information, experiences, drives and motivations that produce distortions and dysfunctions.

144. A: The next priority is to identify and evaluate the antecedents and consequences of the behavior. In this way the social worker and client will be able to revise the antecedents and consequences in such a way as to induce change. In setting goals and measuring progress, the behavior will be need to be operationally defined (i.e., a vague problem, such as aggression, must be made explicit and measurable--frequency of hitting, throwing things, yelling, etc.), thus allowing for the identification of targets for change, quantified goal setting, and setting positive and negative reinforcers. In general, unconscious motivations, drives, and emotions are not seen as relevant to the goal of behavioral change, from a modification standpoint.

145. B: Crisis intervention recognizes the need for immediate, effective intervention, and a five-stage crisis sequence: 1) acknowledgement of the catastrophic/overwhelming event; 2) a sense of profound vulnerability that overmasters the client's usual coping skills; 3) a last straw precipitating event causing the individual to seek help; 4) emotional turmoil and imbalance; and 5) the application of new and/or more effective coping skills leading to adequate adjustment and acceptance.

146. A: His most likely diagnosis is panic disorder. The symptoms of panic are clear, and there is a specific fear (i.e., he is not suffering for a generalized, nonspecific fear). Specific phobia would lead to avoidance and there is no noted compulsion to go with an obsession noted in the prompt. Common treatment medications: Celexa (citalopram), Haldol (haloperidol), Klonopin (clonazepam), Librium (chlordiazepoxide), Paxil (paroxetine), Valium (diazepam), Tofranil (imipramine), and Xanax (alprazolam).

147. C: This approach would be best referred to as the narrative approach. This family therapy approach suggests that behavior change occurs when family members produce alternate narratives, stories, or scenarios with improved endings by which to focus their energies and beliefs in a more positive way. Complementary therapy refers to supplemental intervention(s) that a social worker may use in addition to individual therapy. Collaborative therapy refers to family therapy provided by two or more social workers pursuing the same cooperative goals. The social learning approach seeks to teach family members added skills (conflict resolution, negotiation, communication, etc.) to address and resolve family dysfunction.

148. A: The "Electra Complex" is the female counterpart to the "Oedipus Complex" and typically occurs between the ages of three and seven.

149. C: Strategic family therapy focuses on family rules and behavioral patterns. This approach suggests that persistent behavioral dysfunction and faulty family rules are at the heart of most family problems. Intervention is supplied by the social worker actively choosing to engage the family in ways that will highlight problematic behavioral patterns. In this way the family becomes more aware of problematic patterns of interaction, after which the social worker can assist the family in choosing more functional behaviors and interactive patterns.

150. B: Minority group is a group of individuals with one or more characteristics identified as being subordinately distinct in a larger societal context. Of significance, in the social sciences, a minority group need not be smaller (in terms of population) than a dominant group. Rather it is identified as such because the distinct identifying characteristic(s) put the group in a position of subordinate status in a societal context.

Practice Test #2

1. A social worker has been asked to see a 15-year-old girl for problems with body image and eating. After speaking with her, the social worker discovers that she suffers with an intense desire to lose weight, feeling that this will help her be more attractive to the opposite sex and more popular in her social circle. She is by no means obese or even "chubby" although she is not overly slender. Her parents recently noted an increase in grocery costs, and that food seemed to be disappearing around the house inordinately quickly—often "junk" food and other quick snacks. Finally, late one night, her mother passed the bathroom and heard the daughter "purge" her food. She confronted her and discovered that the daughter had been "binge" eating and inducing vomiting for some months. She estimates that she purges about 10 times per week. Some modest weight loss had occurred. The most appropriate diagnosis would be:

a. Anorexia nervosa, purging type.
b. Bulimia nervosa, severe.
c. Bulimia nervosa, moderate.
d. Eating disorder, not otherwise specified.

2. A social worker sees a mother with a child recently diagnosed with juvenile onset diabetes. She is stressed and feels overwhelmed with and uncertain of the requirements of caring for this child's new special needs. This parent would best be served by joining which type of group?

a. An educational group
b. A support group
c. A self-help group
d. A task group

3. A social worker is called to see a young black man in his mid-twenties. Two adult sisters brought him for an urgent appointment. The young man is clean, neatly dressed in slacks, dress shoes, and a tweed sport coat. He is also calm, relaxed, and without any signs of agitation. The two sisters, however, appear disheveled, frazzled, and almost histrionic. They blurt out the he "has problems" and urge the social worker to talk with him. Privately, he tells the social worker that he is fine. Later, however, the ladies tell the social worker he left home abruptly and traveled cross-country with no destination. He didn't sleep for three days (with them pursuing him), was spending money excessively and writing checks he couldn't cover. He ended up in a nationally famous amusement park at 3:00 a.m. (having scaled a fence), sitting on an empty rollercoaster "waiting for the ride to start." When confronted, he admits all of this, but says he's now rested, and doing better. The most likely diagnosis would be:

a. Brief psychotic disorder.
b. Bipolar I, manic episode, with psychotic features, in full remission.
c. Bipolar I, hypomanic episode, in full remission.
d. Cyclothymic disorder.

4. Bloom's taxonomy outlines behaviors necessary for learning. Which 3 kinds of learning does the theory describe?

a. Cognitive, affective, and psychomotor
b. Auditory, visual, and kinesthetic
c. Formal and informal
d. Attitudes, subjective norms, and behavioral intention

5. Personality disorders are pervasive and enduring patterns of dysfunction. The DSM provides for the diagnosis of ten specific personality disorders, and one category for indeterminate behaviors that appear to characteristic of a personality disorder. These disorders are grouped into three clusters. Which of the following clusters does not properly describe a personality disorder group?

a. Cluster B: Paranoid, Schizoid, and Schizotypal Disorders (also referred to as "odd or eccentric behavior disorders")
b. Cluster B: Impulsivity and/or Affective Dysregulation Disorders (also referred to as "dramatic, emotional, or erratic disorders")
c. Cluster B: Violent and/or Explosive Disorders (also referred to as "aggressive and intrusive conduct disorders")
d. Cluster C: Anxiety and Compulsive Disorders (also referred to as "anxious or fearful disorders")

6. The "5 rights of delegation" include:

a. right time, right place, right person, right direction, and right evaluation.
b. right person, right place, right time, right assignment, and right supervision.
c. right task, right time, right circumstance, right place, and right supervision.
d. right task, right circumstance, right person, right direction, and right supervision.

7. A school counselor is scheduled to see a 9-year-old boy regarding disruptive behavior in the classroom. Rather than begin with an office visit, the counselor directly observes his behavior in the classroom. There the counselor noted the following: he seemed to constantly fidget and squirm in his seat; he talked nonstop; he was frequently out of his seat, running, touching, and playing with anything and everything he could reach. The teacher's efforts to quiet him appeared to be forgotten almost instantly. When an art period was begun, which engaged most children, he still had difficulty as he was easily distracted and seemed to switch constantly from one activity to another. He appeared unable to slow down long enough to receive even simple and clear instructions. The few moments he was quiet, he seemed lost in daydreaming, staring out the classroom windows. The most likely diagnosis for this youngster is:

a. Attention deficit hyperactivity disorder (AD/HD)
b. Conduct disorder.
c. Obsessive compulsive disorder.
d. Oppositional defiant disorder.

8. Failing to provide reasonable care based upon appropriate standards and expertise is an example of:

a. laziness.
b. poor judgment.
c. negligent conduct.
d. inadequate supervision.

9. The perspective from which a social worker approaches client interactions should be based upon a blend of: 1) time and resources available; 2) the treatment modality required (individual, family, group); 3) the issues to be addressed; 4) the outcomes (goals) sought; and 5) an appropriate theoretical framework. Taken together, this defines the social worker's:

a. theoretical orientation.
b. practice framework.
c. clinical approach.
d. model of interaction.

10. A social worker notices that the waiting area outside the pediatric intensive care unit is frequently filled with parents talking and sharing together. Over time it becomes apparent that there is an informal structure to the group, and considerable information is being exchanged (some accurate, some not). The social worker recognizes this group structure as a:

a. formed group.
b. natural group.
c. closed group.
d. structured group.

11. A practice framework that acknowledges and accounts for a client's overall context in: 1) social setting (family, peers, neighborhood, etc.); 2) social relations quality (e.g., with other family members, friends, coworkers, etc.); 3) external pressures (work, organizations, etc.); 4) culture; and 5) life-course events (marriage, births, retirement, etc.) is called a(n):

a. ecosystems framework.
b. cultural framework.
c. strengths framework.
d. generalist framework.

12. During an interview with a patient, what type of patient response provides the most useful information about the patient?

a. Verbal responses
b. Non-verbal responses
c. Silence
d. Both verbal and non-verbal responses

13. A practice framework that approaches a client's issue or presenting problem from the perspective of gender, sex roles, and related stereotyping and discrimination, along with the influence that these elements may bring to bear on the issue or presenting problem, is called a:

a. gender framework.
b. roles framework.
c. strengths framework.
d. feminist framework.

14. Providing professional guidance and being someone to whom other staff can bring questions or concerns may be described as:

a. mentoring.
b. role modeling.
c. supervising.
d. coaching.

15. A practice framework that approaches a client's issue or presenting problem with particular sensitivity and attention to culture, ethnicity, and/or religion (or other similar perspective that is integral to the client's definition of self) is called a(n):

a. cultural framework.
b. systems framework.
c. ethnic-sensitive framework.
d. strengths framework.

16. The best determinant of the effectiveness of patient education is:
   a. patient satisfaction.
   b. a patient's ability to demonstrate a procedure.
   c. a patient's ability to explain a procedure and demonstrate understanding.
   d. a patient's behavior modification and compliance rates.

17. A therapeutic approach that views the client from a social context, that sees behavior as derived from unconscious drives and motivations, that views disorders and dysfunction as emerging from internal conflicts and anxiety, and that seeks to facilitate the conscious awareness of previously repressed information is called a:
   a. cognitive approach.
   b. psychoanalytic approach.
   c. Gestalt approach.
   d. behavior approach.

18. Which right is included in the Patients' Bill of Rights?
   a. Affordable healthcare
   b. Pain control
   c. Right to sue
   d. Access to latest medical technology

19. If a client has difficulty working with a particular social worker because the social worker reminds her of her father, and the social worker is struggling to work well with the client because she has strong traits reminiscent of those of his ex-spouse, the client and the social worker (respectively) are experiencing issues known as:
   a. individuation/separation conflicts.
   b. separation/individuation conflicts.
   c. transference/countertransference conflicts.
   d. countertransference/transference conflicts.

20. Jamie is being counseled to aid in dealing with her fear of intimacy. During a session, the social worker notes that whenever her mother's name is mentioned, Jamie's responses become shorter and she quickly changes the subject. What should the social worker do?
   a. Increase Jamie's comfort level by avoiding the subject of her mother
   b. Focus attention on the issue of Jamie's mother
   c. Ignore the mother issue, as it's not significant
   d. Use the mother issue to springboard into gaining more information about other family members

21. Collectively, the elements of engagement (building rapport, trust, etc.), contracting (identifying goals and responsibilities), treatment processes, and termination (reviewing goals achieved and ways to independently further progress, etc.) are known as:
   a. the phases of treatment.
   b. the counseling process.
   c. the therapeutic process.
   d. collaborative problem-solving.

22. Which of these efforts is NOT integral in effective group leadership?

a. Consciously using body language to facilitate communication and openness
b. Preserving an effective, safe, and nurturing group environment (ensuring quality information is shared, dispelling myths, deflecting ganging up, pairing, scapegoating, and clique [subgroup] development by some members, etc.)
c. Unconditional positive regard for and non-judgmental acceptance of group members
d. Recruiting membership to ensure a large and diverse population, ideally consisting of more than 20 group members

23. A therapeutic approach that views issues of dysfunction from the perspective of behavior (as opposed to emotional and mental problems), and that discounts delving into past history and unconscious motivations in favor of conditioning, reinforcement, consequences, and conscious choice would best be referred to as a:

a. Gestalt approach.
b. cognitive approach.
c. behavioral approach.
d. task-centered approach.

24. A legal document that specifically designates someone to make decisions regarding medical and end-of-life care if a patient is mentally incompetent is a(n):

a. advance directive.
b. Do-not-resuscitate order.
c. Durable Power of Attorney for Health Care.
d. general power of attorney.

25. A therapeutic approach that views thoughts and cognition as directly responsible for emotions and behaviors, that sees the change of false beliefs and misconceptions as the primary task, that is highly problem-focused and goal-directed, and that is oriented toward the here and now (as opposed to the past) is best described as a:

a. task-centered approach.
b. crisis intervention approach.
c. Gestalt approach.
d. cognitive approach.

26. A social worker has been assigned to chair a task group. The most effective way of organizing the work of the group is by FIRST:

a. agreeing to a consensus form of decision-making
b. specifying the group's objectives
c. rotating the role of facilitator among group members
d. specifying the group's timeline

27. Treatment concepts and techniques such as dream analysis, exploration of the past, free association (saying anything that comes to mind in order to explore unconscious thoughts), ventilation, sustainment (encouragement, reassurance, etc.), confrontation (to overcome "resistance"), and direct influence (advice and direction) are all associated with:

a. behavioral modification.
b. psychoanalysis.
c. Gestalt therapy.
d. cognitive therapy.

28. Jung's theory about development of the personality over the lifespan is referred to as:

a. hierarchy of needs.
b. theory of individualism.
c. age stratification.
d. life course.

29. Treatment concepts and techniques such as identification of target behaviors, antecedents, reinforcers (positive and negative), consequences, etc., along with tracking mechanisms (tally sheets, charts, etc.), journal-keeping regarding specific occurrences (when, where, with whom, etc.), and related feelings (including intensity, frequency, etc.) are all associated with:

a. behavioral therapy.
b. Gestalt therapy.
c. psychoanalytic therapy.
d. cognitive therapy.

30. A social worker has been moderating a closed membership growth group and notices group members seem to be expressing more diverse opinions among themselves. This is an indication that the group has entered which stage of group development?

a. Stage 3: Intimacy
b. Stage 5: Separation
c. Stage 4: Differentiation
d. Stage 2: Power and control

31. Treatment concepts and techniques such as clarification (feedback and illumination of misconceptions), explanation (education regarding misconceptions, thought "triggers" and secondary thoughts, beliefs, and actions), interpretation (insight development), paradoxical direction (having the client engage or continue behaviors needing correction to enhance awareness and induce a sense of control), reflection (reviewing), and writing (diagramming misconceptions and analyzing thoughts, etc.) are all associated with:

a. Gestalt therapy.
b. psychoanalytic therapy.
c. cognitive therapy.
d. task-centered therapy.

32. One advantage of group instruction over one-on-one instruction is:

a. it is more cost-effective.
b. it requires less planning.
c. it allows more time for questions.
d. it is more flexible.

33. A therapeutic approach that teaches a phenomenological method of awareness, with a focus on immediate perceptions, feelings, and actions as separate from interpreting and recapitulating preexisting attitudes, and where explanations and interpretations are set aside in favor of what is directly perceived and felt is called:

a. cognitive therapy.
b. psychoanalytic therapy.
c. task-centered therapy.
d. Gestalt therapy.

34. A social worker notices that when working with clients who have health complaints, he experiences emotional irritation and has little patience for encouraging such discussion. What should the social worker do?

a. Nothing, as every social worker has points of irritation
b. Self-examine to determine possible reasons for the reaction
c. Take steps to ensure that he no longer treats clients of this type
d. Report the difficulty immediately to his supervisor

35. A therapeutic approach that focuses solely on changing behaviors and issues that the client (as opposed to the social worker) believes to be problematic, and that views behaviors as fully conscious acts, and that views individuals as fully able to control their actions and make needed changes is called:

a. crisis intervention.
b. task-centered therapy.
c. psychoanalytic therapy.
d. cognitive therapy.

36. Pain Assessment in Advanced Dementia (PAINAD) utilizes:

a. a face scale with pictures of smiling or crying faces.
b. a "0" (no pain) to "10" (severe pain) scale.
c. monitoring of blood pressure changes.
d. observations of non-verbal behavior.

37. Treatment concepts and techniques such as "dialogue" (using the "empty chair" technique – i.e., talking with an absent person to reveal inner conflicts), "enactment of dreams," "exaggeration" (dramatizing a physical or verbal action in order to enhance awareness), "exposure of the obvious" (also to enhance client awareness), and "rehearsal" (practicing feelings, thoughts, and behaviors in preparation for change) are used to engage and overcome barriers such as "confluence" (a preoccupation with false similarities while ignoring or denying differences), "introjection" (an over-identification and integration of messages from others), "projection" (attributing one's own dysfunctional personality traits to others), and "retroflection" (doing to oneself what one wishes to do to another), which are all associated with:

a. task-centered therapy.
b. crisis intervention.
c. Gestalt therapy.
d. behavioral therapy.

38. The Confusion Assessment Method is a tool that covers 9 factors related to mental status. This tool is used to assess for:

a. delirium.
b. Alzheimer's disease.
c. substance abuse.
d. brain injury.

39. A therapeutic approach that sees periods of intense trauma as optimal for effecting change, and that seeks to equip clients with new and/or more effective coping skills to manage traumatic situations is known as:

a. cognitive therapy.
b. behavioral therapy.
c. task-centered therapy.
d. crisis intervention.

40. A client's main goal is to be free of conflict when called upon to make a decision. She has suffered for years with being unable to make efficient choices and never again wants to experience anxiety when debating a choice. What is likely to happen in terms of counseling?

a. The client will be happy during the course of counseling
b. Counseling will be of a short-term nature
c. She will effectively meet her therapy goal with time and patience
d. Counseling will become interminable

41. A therapeutic approach that views the family as a central source of strength and support for individuals, that views the family as composed of multiple subsystems (i.e., spousal, parent-child, and sibling subsystems), and views that dysfunction and conflict in any one subsystem can penetrate and affecting the other subsystems is called:

a. family therapy.
b. crisis intervention.
c. systems therapy.
d. behavioral therapy.

42. A problem list focuses on:

a. a prioritized list of patient problems based on assessment, history, and interview.
b. all identified patient problems based on assessment, history, and interview.
c. the patient's self-reported problems.
d. a standardized list of problems related to specific diagnoses.

43. A therapeutic approach that arises from the belief that individual in similar situations can identify with, comfort, reassure, and help one another is called:

a. group therapy.
b. conjoint therapy.
c. collective therapy.
d. systems therapy.

44. Working for the best interests of the patient despite conflicting personal values and assisting patients to have access to appropriate resources may be defined as:

a. moral agency.
b. advocacy.
c. agency.
d. collaboration.

45. The concepts of "preaffiliation" (becoming acquainted), "power and control" (setting the roles), "intimacy" (developing cohesion), "differentiation" (independent opinion expression), and "separation" (moving to closure and termination) are all stages in:

a. the lifecycle of a therapeutic relationship.
b. general relationship cycles.
c. group development.
d. team cohesion.

46. Which therapy involves the use of monitoring devices to allow people to control their own physiological responses?

a. imagery.
b. acupuncture.
c. meditation.
d. biofeedback.

47. Treatment concepts and techniques largely oriented around immediate problem-solving, stress reduction, coping skill enhancement, support system building, and emotional buffering are primarily associated with:

a. grief therapy.
b. crisis intervention.
c. task-centered therapy.
d. short-term therapy.

48. A client has been in therapy for several months because of depression and suicide ideation. Progress has been limited until, during a particular session, the client demonstrates a positive attitude and reports he has "turned a corner" and finally feels relaxed and happy. What should his social worker do?

a. take a position of extreme caution
b. feel good that the client has finally "turned a corner"
c. make plans to terminate counseling because the client has improved
d. continue with counseling as usual

49. Specific treatment approaches, such as the "communications approach" (which sees communication deficits as central to interpersonal dysfunction), the "structural approach" (which views interpersonal interactions as central to dysfunction), the "social learning approach" (focusing on improving interactive skills such as conflict resolution and communication), and the "narrative approach" (using personal stories, ideas, thoughts, etc., and revisions, to discover and implement new behavior patterns) are associated with:

a. group therapy.
b. cognitive therapy.
c. behavioral therapy.
d. family therapy.

50. A client is the same gender as the social worker and not homosexual. The client is seeing the social worker because of relationship issues. During the course of treatment, it becomes apparent that the client is directing feelings of a romantic nature toward the social worker. What is likely to be the cause of the client's feelings?

a. An unhealthy attachment to the social worker
b. A genuine romantic attraction to the social worker
c. Transference
d. None of the above

51. All of the following are kinds of group therapy structures EXCEPT:

a. natural groups (groups which coalesce independently, and seek a moderator only later – such as a divorce group).
b. formed groups (groups formed around a specific issue or to achieve a certain goal).
c. forced groups (groups arising from court orders, insurance mandates, or other criteria requiring attendance).
d. short-term groups (groups oriented around a crisis situation [e.g., hospitalization of a loved one] or other short-term event, such as birth preparation, etc.).

52. The best approach to solving a problem that involves 3 different departments in a hospital is:

a. forming an interdisciplinary team that works together to find a solution.
b. the administration resolves the problem independently.
c. each department proposes a solution to administration.
d. all three departments have a joint meeting to brainstorm possible solutions.

53. The following five stage sequence is reflective of a therapeutic modality: 1) a significant stressor or disastrous event; 2) an increase in vulnerability and anxiety (escalating when coping skills are overwhelmed); 3) a "last straw" event that motivates help seeking; 4) a period of turmoil and confusion; and 5) the use of new coping skills, coupled with acceptance and accommodation of change. The therapeutic modality is:

a. cognitive therapy.
b. crisis intervention.
c. behavioral therapy.
d. psychoanalytic therapy.

54. Clients have an ethical right to self-determination. When may a social worker limit this right?

a. When there's a threat to self or others
b. If the client is choosing poorly
c. When the courts are involved
d. If the client's family is opposed to a particular action

55. According to Kübler-Ross, individuals typically pass through five stages of grief to reconcile a loss. Those stages, in order, are:

a. Anger, denial, bargaining, despair/depression, acceptance.
b. Denial, anger, bargaining, despair/depression, acceptance.
c. Denial, anger, despair/depression, bargaining, acceptance.
d. Anger, bargaining, denial, despair/depression, acceptance.

56. When preparing written materials for patients, what readability level would be appropriate for a homogeneous adult patient group in an affluent area?

a. Grade 6 level
b. Grade 9 level
c. Grade 3 level
d. Grade 12 level

57. A theoretical approach that believes that individuals, families, and groups are all part of a greater whole, with "boundaries" (invisible lines of separation) between each, that change in any one will result in change in the others, and that "entropy" describes the de-organization of any or all of these parts of the whole, but which notes that they tend toward "homeostatic balance" and resist entropy, is called:

a. integration theory.
b. group theory.
c. holistic theory.
d. systems theory.

58. Which of Piaget's stages of cognitive development is characterized by the ability to think logically, use abstraction, and test hypotheses?

a. Sensorimotor
b. Preoperational, preconceptual, and intuitive
c. Concrete operational
d. Formal operational

59. A theoretical approach that focuses on the relationship between living things and their social and physical environment, that sees "adaptation" as the process by which individuals and environments accommodate each other in seeking a "goodness of fit," and that views dysfunction as a failure to cooperate and accommodate is called:

a. systems theory.
b. ecosystems theory.
c. ecological theory.
d. conservation theory.

60. A team leader makes decisions independently and strictly enforces all rules. This type of leadership is:

a. bureaucratic.
b. laissez-faire.
c. autocratic.
d. democratic.

61. A therapeutic approach that involves "field theory" (where everything that happens is interrelated through a larger network of interactions, and can only be fully understood in the context of the interrelatedness), "figure/ground formation" (which suggests that whatever is most important in the here and now becomes figural and invites attention, leaving everything else to drift into the background), exploration of "resistances," the processing of "introjects" (messages internalized in childhood), and the use of "experiments" to increase awareness and growth is called:

a. existential theory.
b. cognitive theory.
c. Gestalt theory.
d. systems theory.

62. The manner of making eye contact, the tone of voice, along with touch, gestures, and posture are examples of:

a. non-verbal communication.
b. therapeutic communication.
c. proxemics.
d. non-therapeutic communication.

63. A therapeutic approach that focuses on the multidimensional aspects of the individual (interpersonal, psychological, social, and environmental), and that engages the client in the context of his or her personal history, strengths, weaknesses, resources, wants, and needs is referred to as:

a. cognitive therapy.
b. lifecourse therapy.
c. psychoanalytic therapy.
d. psychosocial therapy.

64. In the course of explaining her marital problems, a client also alludes to various symptoms that could be diagnosed as psychotic in nature. Her social worker doesn't have training in psychosis and should:

a. continue to work with the client but research psychosis.
b. consult with a social worker trained in psychosis.
c. discontinue counseling and refer the client to another social worker.
d. discontinue counseling because the social worker isn't qualified in this case.

65. A therapeutic approach that assumes clients to be competent to co-construct goals and strategies (and that resistance is lowest when clients are conscripted in co-formulating interventions); that views that clients are experts regarding their own lives and experience meanings; that encourages change by "doing something differently", even while recognizing that only small steps need be taken (as change often "snowballs" and grows naturally); and that suggests "if it isn't broken, don't fix it" and "if it didn't work, try something different" is called:

a. solution-focused therapy.
b. cognitive therapy.
c. problem-oriented therapy.
d. systems therapy.

66. Which of the following most closely characterizes Selye's biological theory of stress and aging?

a. The body is a machine that wears out over time
b. The body's response to stress is characterized by a generalized adaptation syndrome
c. All cells and organisms have a programmed life span
d. Over time, mutations occur that interfere with body functioning and cause aging

67. A therapeutic approach that is used primarily with the elderly and with those experiencing loss (e.g., disability, bereavement, unemployment, etc.), is often adjunctive to other therapeutic interventions that focus on important survivor questions (What is the meaning of life? Why go on? What have I accomplished? How well did I utilize life's opportunities? Etc.), and that see three key paths to meaning (creativity, experiential values [finding beauty], and attitudinal values [a posture toward positive coping]) is called:

a. group therapy.
b. logotherapy.
c. psychosocial therapy.
d. crisis intervention.

68. A client reveals to his social worker that he has recently entered into a business relationship with the social worker's spouse. Is this likely to present a concern?

a. Yes, but only if the counseling relationship has just begun
b. Yes, but only if money is involved
c. Yes, under all circumstances
d. No

69. A therapeutic approach that is based on "fundamental units of social intercourse" and "fundamental units of social action" (called "strokes"), carried out through stimulus-response patterns (including words, tones, and expressions) mediated by "ego states" (the "parent" [concepts taught before age five], the "child" [feelings derived before age five], and the "adult" [learned concepts from childhood onward]), and framed in the belief of individual value, a capacity to think, and the ability to change is called:

a. social therapy.
b. psychosocial therapy.
c. cognitive therapy.
d. transactional analysis.

70. A social worker has recently entered into a counseling relationship with a client who has a past history of depression and suicide attempts. The social worker will want to give particular care to discussing:

a. the limits of confidentiality
b. the legal definition of suicide
c. his experience in treating patients who are depressed
d. the effects of suicide upon family and friends

71. There are two forms of conditioning that can be used to modify behavior. One form of conditioning is used to train autonomic responses and to associate a stimulus that normally wouldn't have any effect with a stimulus that would. The second form of conditioning creates an association between a behavior and a consequence (also called "response-stimulus" conditioning). In the order presented here, name these two forms of conditioning:

a. autonomic conditioning and learned conditioning.
b. neurological conditioning and cognitive conditioning.
c. classical conditioning and operant conditioning.
d. trained conditioning and planned conditioning.

72. A client wants to read his personal records. What should the social worker do?

a. Deny the request and explain that records are private
b. Provide the records and help to interpret them
c. Allow the client to see only those parts that are pertinent
d. Deny the request

73. A client who previously met the criteria for tobacco use disorder has not smoked in 10 weeks. He is using a nicotine replacement system, NicoDerm CQ. The client has not had any symptoms of tobacco use disorder except craving. This client should be considered:

a. not in remission, due to using a nicotine replacement medication.
b. in early remission.
c. not in remission, due to symptoms of tobacco use disorder.
d. not in remission, due to not meeting timeframe for remission.

74. The term "correlation" refers to the relationship of the sample variables to each other. This relationship is expressed via a "correlation coefficient" (symbolized as "r"). A perfect correlation (where all measurement points between two variables coincide) is statistically represented by the following correlation coefficient value:

a. 1.0.
b. 9.9.
c. 0.0.
d. 0.5.

75. An individual with whom a social worker has had a previous sexual relationship has arrived in her office seeking counseling for an addiction problem. What should the social worker do?

a. Begin counseling, because the relationship is in the past
b. Enter into a co-therapy situation
c. Design a treatment plan but refer to a colleague
d. Refer the client to another social worker

76. Following the death of a young child from cancer, a couple comes in for help in resolving complicated feelings of grief. When the couple enters the office, the social worker notes that both the husband and wife pull their chairs slightly away from each other and make no verbal, physical, or eye-contact. The social worker's best response would be to:

a. ignore the behavior.
b. explicitly address and explore the behavior.
c. mention the behavior casually.
d. confront the couple about the behavior.

77. Assessment of a substance user should always include: 1) kind of substance used; 2) frequency and quantity of use; 3) typical level of intoxication; 4) withdrawal symptom severity (if experienced); 5) duration of substance abuse (months or years, etc.); 6) mode of use (oral, inhalation, needles, etc.); 7) any related legal history; 8) comprehensive history of any prior treatment (length, voluntary/involuntary; type and methods of treatment, successful or unsuccessful program completion). All of the following should also be included EXCEPT:

a. family history of substance abuse/use.
b. social history.
c. impact of use on daily living.
d. sources where substances were obtained.

78. Five specific elements (1) a research hypothesis; 2) a null hypothesis; 3) a test statistic; 4) a rejection region; and 5) a conclusion) collectively make up what is called a:

a. theoretical construct.
b. conceptual construct.
c. statistical paradigm.
d. statistical test.

79. All of the following represent treatment modalities for substance abuse EXCEPT:

a. detoxification (ridding the body of toxins that have accumulated from drug use – which may or may not be medically supervised).
b. pharmacologic treatment (to reduce withdrawal symptoms or to induce abuser avoidant-reactions in an effort to reduce future substance abuse).
c. drug "affinity" testing to determine the level of addiction present.
d. psychosocial treatment (counseling and behavior modification, group therapy, etc.) to help establish new coping skills.

80. During an initial session with a client, it becomes apparent that the client is reluctant to disclose his primary problem. Which of the following approaches would be the least effective in overcoming the client's reluctance?

a. Developing a written contract based on specific goals and expected outcomes
b. Simply asking the client directly why he/she is unwilling to cooperate
c. Addressing the anticipated number of sessions, meeting frequency and duration, and the costs involved
d. Openly acknowledging the client's reluctance to open up and share information

81. Cognitive-behavioral therapy is the most commonly used approach to substance abuse treatment. Also used, however, is behavioral therapy, group and family therapy, and all of the following EXCEPT:

a. psychodynamic therapy
b. psychoanalytic therapies.
c. self-help groups.
d. interventional therapies.

82. The term referring to the threshold necessary to decide whether an intervention produced an outcome, or whether it was the result of chance is "statistical significance." The actual value threshold indicating reasonable probability that the intervention produced an outcome is called the "level of significance." An acceptable probability that the null hypothesis will be incorrectly rejected (a type I error) is traditionally placed at 0.5. Where greater certitude is required, it may be placed at 0.1. This threshold value is properly referred to as a study's:

a. alpha value.
b. beta value.
c. kappa value.
d. omega value.

83. The scope of substance abuse treatment varies in accordance with numerous factors. In particular, individuals requiring a medically supervised detoxification period, individuals who have overdosed, individuals who had received unsuccessful treatment in the past, and those with psychiatric disorders require more intensive interventions, potentially including hospitalization. Others may benefit from residential treatment programs that help them to stay away from the drug of abuse until they are better able to assert personal control. Studies indicate that the minimum time period in a residential program to achieve better long-term outcomes is:

a. 30 days (one month).
b. 90 days (three months).
c. 180 days (six months).
d. 365 days (12 months).

84. A male client tells a female social worker that he just cannot speak with a woman and requests assignment to a male social worker. The social worker's best response would be to:

a. aid the client in exploring his difficulties in this area.
b. explain that this should not be a problem.
c. promptly terminate the relationship.
d. arrange a case transfer or referral.

85. Substance-related disorders may be grouped into 10 "classes" such as: 1) alcohol; 2) cannabis; 3) tobacco; 4) hallucinogens; 5) narcotics; 6) stimulants; 7) caffeine 8) inhalants 9) opioids 10) sedatives, hypnotics, and anxiolytics. Please classify cocaine (and the freebased form, crack cocaine) into the proper category, among which one of the following classes?

a. Opioids
b. Hallucinogen
c. Narcotic
d. Stimulant

86. Social service programs can be categorized in all of the following ways EXCEPT:

a. exceptional eligibility programs.
b. means tested programs.
c. universal programs.
d. selective eligibility programs.

87. Most anxiolytics are a subclass of what drug classification?

a. Hallucinogens
b. Stimulants
c. Depressants
d. Narcotics

88. Extensive patient and caregiver participation in interdisciplinary team discussions is important so that the:

a. patient and caregivers can be informed of the plan of care as formulated by the medical providers.
b. cost of hospice care is reimbursed by the patient's insurance provider.
c. plan of care can be crafted to meet the specific needs and goals of the individual patient and family.
d. patient and caregivers come to terms with a terminal prognosis.

89. Communication is most broadly defined as:

a. verbal expressions between two or more individuals.
b. body language (facial expressions, gestures, posture, signals, etc.) conveying meaning between two or more individuals.
c. written expressions shared between two or more individuals.
d. all of the above.

90. The social security program was enacted in 1935 to provide "old age survivors benefits." Individuals who are employed and paying into the social security system can earn up to four tax credits annually. To be eligible to receive social security retirement benefits, an individual must have earned a lifetime credit total of at least:

a. 80 credits.
b. 60 credits.
c. 40 credits.
d. 20 credits.

91. Significant client factors that may influence the communication process include: 1) age; 2) education; 3) ethnicity; 4) culture (and belief systems); 5) ethnicity; 6) primary language; and all of the following EXCEPT:

a. grooming and hygiene.
b. emotional state.
c. intellectual level.
d. gender.

92. A female patient scheduled for a surgical procedure is a Jehovah's Witness. What aspect of future care could be affected by the patient's religious practices?

a. Diet
b. Covering of body with a burka
c. Organ donation
d. Blood transfusion

93. When exploring a client's concerns, he begins to divulge important personal information about his marital situation. At one point he seems to be having difficulty finding adequate words to express his emotions, fears, and concerns. After two or three efforts to express a particularly sensitive issue, he seems unable to find the words to continue and a long pause ensues. At this juncture the social worker should:

a. attempt to further the discussion by suggesting what he might have been trying to say.
b. press the client to continue so as not to lose the momentum of the conversation.
c. discuss with him the difficulty he is experiencing, and encourage him to take more time.
d. ignore the pause and remain quiet no matter how long it takes.

94. Publicly funded disability insurance is available to individuals who become unemployable due to a permanent or chronic disability. At a minimum, the disability must be expected to last for a year or more, or be expected to result in death. This program is administered by:

a. each state's Department of Human Services.
b. the federal Department of Health and Human Services.
c. the federal Disabled Persons Program.
d. the Social Security Administration.

95. A social worker meets a client, and discovers that she has limited English-speaking skills. The social worker has some ability to speak her primary language, but is not fluent. At this point the social worker should:

a. terminate the meeting immediately, until it can be arranged for her to see a social worker who speaks her native language.
b. revise the meeting to cover only very basic issues until other arrangements can be made.
c. delay the meeting to find an interpreter before continuing.
d. attempt to interview her in her own language.

96. A client is seen who is in a verbally abusive relationship. She admits that he has been verbally abused, including frequent angry outbursts, routine put-downs, and name-calling. Friends and relatives have encouraged her to end the relationship, but she continues to struggle with intense feelings of attachment and affection for him. The first step should be to:

a. confront the client with the reality of the abuse.
b. acknowledge the highly ambivalent feelings she is experiencing.
c. offer reading material on abusive relationships.
d. explore the client's other relationships, past and present.

97. Asking the question "why" can be problematic because:

a. the client may feel the inquiry is intrusive.
b. the question may seem confrontational.
c. the client may feel at fault for a lack of clarity.
d. the client may feel judged or challenged in his response.

98. A social insurance program for individuals sustaining employment-related injuries is the:

a. Employee Assistance Program.
b. State Compensation Program.
c. Worker's Compensation Program.
d. Worker's Health Program.

99. When using "active" or "reflective" listening, "furthering responses" (short verbal or non-verbal cues to continue) can be used to ease the conversation along while helping the client to feel fully heard. All of the following are examples of furthering responses EXCEPT:

a. "Okay" declarations.
b. head nodding.
c. "Go on" insertions.
d. "Um-hmm" or "yes" interjections.

100. A client seems to frequently have difficulty formulating her thoughts. She pauses often, partially completes her sentences, presents as somewhat helpless and needy, and seems openly eager for the social worker to do most of the talking. The most appropriate response for the social worker would be to:

a. take over and lecture the client about her life.
b. confront the client and demand that she talk more openly.
c. use reflective listening techniques and allow the client more time.
d. stop talking and use silence aggressively to stimulate discussion.

101. The difference between "rephrasing" and "paraphrasing" what a client has said is:

a. rephrasing is used to correct what the client said wrong, while paraphrasing is used to repeat the same idea back.
b. rephrasing is used to elaborate on what the client said, while paraphrasing is used to reiterate it.
c. rephrasing is used to emphasize what the client said, while paraphrasing is used to show mutual understanding.
d. rephrasing is used to clarify what the client said, while paraphrasing is used to explain what the client said.

102. The government has established a "poverty line" threshold regarding income. Individuals who fall below that threshold may be eligible for means-tested public assistance. Eligible individuals include the "working poor," as well as individuals who are elderly, disabled, and/or blind. Primarily funded by the federal government, benefits are also supplemented by the state. This program is called the:

a. Indigent and Poverty Program.
b. Supplemental Security Income program.
c. Income and Poverty Assistance Program.
d. Security and Stability Income Program.

103. Active or "reflective" listening includes the use of attending non-verbal cues (sitting forward, making good eye contact, using content-appropriate affective expressions, etc.), as well as all of the following EXCEPT:

a. clarification ("Are you saying...?").
b. substitution ("What I would do is...").
c. encouragement ("Tell me more" and "Go on").
d. summarization ("What you're saying is...").

104. Symbols of alcohol misuse include all of the following EXCEPT:

a. involuntary defecation.
b. respiratory depression.
c. excessive energy.
d. confusion/disorientation.

105. Leading questions tend to stifle communication, and usually result in closed-ended ("yes" or "no" short-answer) responses. All of the following are examples of "leading questions" EXCEPT:

a. "You do know...[a certain fact]...don't you?"
b. "Could you tell me more about...[a situation]...?"
c. "But sure you wouldn't want to...[conclusion]...would you?"
d. "I think that...[decision]...would be best, don't you?"

106. In 1966 the program known as "Aid for Families with Dependent Children (AFDC)" was renamed and revised to be a transitional program from welfare to work. The new name of this program is now the:

a. Transitional Aid to Work Program (TAW) program.
b. Family Welfare Resource Transition (FWRT) program.
c. Temporary Assistance for Needy Families (TANF) program.
d. Transitional Aid for Families and Children (TAFC) program.

107. A question that contains multiple parts, potentially leaving a client confused or unclear what the question was, or at least uncertain which part to answer first, is known as a:

a. stacked or complex question
b. manifold question
c. multipart question
d. fragmented or fractured question

108. Which of the following medications are NOT indicated to treat the psychotic symptoms of schizophrenia?

a. Prozax
b. Haldol
c. Thorazine
d. Clorazil

109. When a client seems overwhelmed or uncertain how to share further, it can help to break down the concerns at hand into smaller, more manageable parts. This communication technique is known as:

a. fragmentation.
b. sequestration.
c. downsizing.
d. partialization.

110. The federal health insurance program for the elderly is known as Medicare. Exclusively for individuals over the age of 65 or the disabled, or individuals with end-stage renal disease (ESRD), this insurance has which two specific components?

a. Medical insurance and hospital insurance
b. Physician insurance and hospital insurance
c. Medical insurance and drug coverage
d. Hospital insurance and drug coverage

111. The relationship between a social worker and a client should best be characterized as:

a. a friendship.
b. a peer relationship.
c. a professional relationship.
d. a collegial relationship.

112. Only one of the following food assistance and nutrition programs is not funded by the federal government. The locally funded program is the:

a. Elderly Nutrition Program.
b. Food Stamps Program.
c. Women, Infants, and Children (WIC) program.
d. Meals on Wheels program.

113. A social worker may be required to assume many roles. These include: 1) administrator; 2) advocate; 3) broker (resources and linkages); 4) case manager (resource and service coordinator); 5) counselor; and all of the following EXCEPT:

a. educator and teacher.
b. enforcer and regulator.
c. lobbyist and politician.
d. staff development coordinator.

114. According to Freud's Structural Theory of Personality Development, which part of the personality would be driving the behavior of a serial rapist?

a. The Ego Ideal
b. The Ego
c. The Id
d. The Superego

115. The social work profession is dedicated to meeting basic human needs and enhancing human well-being from a social context, including societal and environmental forces that bear on problems in everyday life. This is/these are the National Association of Social Workers (NASW) social work:

a. creed.
b. goals.
c. vision.
d. primary mission.

116. The concepts of "oral," "anal," "phallic," "latency," and "genital" hierarchically represent:

a. various driving forces of the personality.
b. psychosexual stages of development.
c. terms indicating stages of repression.
d. facets of the personality.

117. Competence, individual dignity, integrity, quality human relationships, service, and social justice are:

a. social work's core values.
b. professional guidelines.
c. therapeutic criteria.
d. social work's goals.

118. Erikson proposed eight psychosocial stages of development. Each stage builds on the other, and to successfully pass through any given stage, one must encounter and overcome a "psychosocial crisis." The crisis arises between two opposing personality features—one that is in harmony with one's personality and one that is not. Erikson called these two opposing features:

a. the Id and Ego.
b. the Yin and Yang.
c. ego-Positive and Ego-Negative.
d. dystonic and syntonic.

119. If a social worker witnesses, obtains evidence, or reasonably suspects abuse (physical, sexual, emotional, financial) of a child, dependent elder, or a dependent adult, or has reason to believe that a client is a danger to himself or others, confidentiality must be suspended and the issue reported to appropriate authorities based upon the social worker status as a(n):

a. evaluator.
b. case manager.
c. mandated reporter.
d. officer of the state.

120. Heinz Hartmann developed the theory of Ego Psychology to explain how individuals use the Ego portion of personality to accommodate the external environment (either changing the self, or acting upon the environment). He proposed that the ego has how many major functions?

a. 12
b. 24
c. 8
d. 36

121. During a series of home visits with an elderly, demented client, the social worker notes that increasing numbers of persons appear to be living in the home. These include purported "relatives" as well as the boyfriend of a privately hired in-home chore worker. During later visits the social worker notes a wide-screen television in the front room, and a new car in the driveway. He also notes that the client is no longer allowed in the main house, and has been moved out of the master bedroom and into a small back room. Most of her clothes also seemed to have disappeared. What primary form of abuse would the social worker suspect in this situation?

a. Physical abuse
b. Financial abuse
c. Emotional abuse
d. Sexual abuse

122. Hartmann's theory of Ego Psychology drew from and built upon Freud's Psychoanalytic Theory. However, in explaining the origin and functions of the Ego, Hartmann parted ways with Freud in one significant area. He believed that the Id and the Ego are specifically present in:

a. adults, following adequate development.
b. children, from birth forward.
c. adolescents, during pre-adult transitioning.
d. latency-aged children, following adequate development.

123. A social worker's client is a married man who has privately disclosed that he is bisexual. He reveals a lengthy history of sexual liaisons with other men, and most recently has disclosed that he is human immunodeficiency virus (HIV) positive (per repeated confirmatory tests via his primary care physician). During multiple contacts the social worker discovers that he has not disclosed his HIV status to his spouse. When discussing issues of transmission, he specifically notes that he does not use any barrier protection during sexual intercourse. Upon explaining the life-and-death risk to his wife, he still maintains that he won't change this behavior. He first minimizes the risk, and then claims she would "suspect something" if he started using a prophylactic. After lengthy counseling he remains unwilling to either reveal his HIV status or to use protection. According to recent interpretations of the "Tarasoff Case" the social worker's duty now is to:

a. continue this as a priority counseling topic.
b. report the case to the Department of Public Health.
c. contact the client's physician to inform him of the problem.
d. contact the client's wife to inform her of the danger.

124. Another human development theory posits that all individuals are born with a need to develop a sense of self, a sense of others, and to build interpersonal relationships. It theorizes that the sense of self and others will affect all subsequent personal relationships. This theory is called:

a. self-psychology.
b. ego psychology.
c. integrative relations theory.
d. object relations theory.

125. The Federal Privacy Act of 1974 (i.e., PL 93-579) requires that clients be informed: 1) when records about them are being maintained; 2) that they have a right to access these records; 3) that they have a right to copies (provided they bear the costs); and 4) that the records will only be used for the purpose they were created unless they provide written release or consent otherwise. Exceptions include: 1) sharing with agency employees on a "need-to-know" basis; 2) legitimate research, if identifying information is removed; and all of the following EXCEPT:

a. providing information to government agencies for legitimate law-enforcement purposes.
b. responding to a court order or subpoena.
c. publication in a reputable professional journal.
d. responding to an emergency to protect another individual.

126. A defense mechanism that serves to repress, disconnect, or dissociate feelings that seem "dangerous" to psychic well-being is called:

a. regression.
b. isolation.
c. splitting.
d. fragmentation.

127. In 1996, legislation was enacted providing Federal protection for personal health records privacy. The legislation applies to all health care providers, health care clearinghouses, and health plan providers. It sets limits on records disclosure and uses, provides for individual access to medical records, and it establishes the right to receive notices of privacy practices. This legislation is called:

a. The Health Records Privacy Act of 1996 (HRPA).
b. The Health Records Privacy and Accountability Act of 1996 (HRPAA).
c. The Health Insurance Portability and Privacy Act of 1996 (HIPPA)
d. The Health Insurance Portability and Accountability Act of 1996 (HIPAA).

128. The theorist most closely identified with Object Relations Theory is:

a. Margaret Mahler.
b. Rene Spitz.
c. John Bowlby.
d. Heinz Kohut.

129. Malpractice liability generally runs from an agency's Board of Directors, to the director, supervisory staff, and then to the front-line social worker. Employer and supervisor liability accrues under the legal theory of:

a. vicarious liability.
b. hierarchical liability.
c. substitute liability.
d. proxy liability.

130. A client is seeing a social worker for difficulties he's experiencing with family conflicts and discusses his employment in the family business. He comments, "I like working that lousy job with my brother. When all is said and done, I really respect that idiot brother of mine." Which of the following does this comment bring to mind?

a. positive communication
b. Freudian conflict
c. disqualifying communication
d. thought/feeling confusion

131. Information protected by confidentiality principles include(s):

a. information obtained directly from a client.
b. client information obtained from a third party.
c. written records and observations regarding a client.
d. all of the above.

132. According to Lawrence Kohlberg, the stage of development in which an individual fully appreciates the need to conform to social rules and laws is:

a. the Conventional Level, stage 4.
b. the Pre-Conventional Level, stage 2.
c. the Post-Conventional Level, stage 5.
d. the Conventional Level, stage 3.

133. Individuals bound by the principles of confidentiality include social workers, agency administrators and supervisors, and all of the following EXCEPT:

a. agency volunteers.
b. other clients.
c. agency clerical staff.
d. agency consultants.

134. Responses to Pavlovian Classical Conditioning are learned in response to an environmental event (or "stimulus"). The response will either be voluntary or involuntary—also known, respectively, as:

a. explicit or incidental responses.
b. emitted or reflexive responses.
c. determined or spontaneous responses.
d. immediate or delayed responses.

135. A child described as "latency aged" will be between the ages:

a. 12-16 years old.
b. 3-6 years old.
c. 6-12 years old.
d. under three years old.

136. In seeking to overcome problems at the community level or that affect society as a whole, a social worker is functioning as a(n):

a. advocate.
b. broker.
c. educator/teacher.
d. lobbyist or politician.

137. At times the social worker may serve as a "case manager." This is because of which part of the social worker's role?

a. Facilitates staff development by means of case presentations
b. Teaches clients tools and strategies for improved functioning
c. Connects clients to needed resources and services and coordinates the delivery and application of these resources and services
d. Implements agency or organizational policies, services and programs

138. A social worker is asked to officiate at a funeral (i.e., introduce speakers and music, and offer closing remarks) for a client who recently died from a brain tumor. She agrees, knowing that the client had few living relatives and friends who could provide this service. Some days after the funeral, a thank-you card arrives. It contains a note of appreciation and a $100.00 bill. The BEST response would be to:

a. graciously accept the money and send a return note of thanks.
b. donate the funds to the local Brain Tumor foundation, thanking them for the funds and telling the family where they were sent.
c. return the money to the family with apologies and explaining that agency policy does not allow social worker's to accept such a substantial gift.
d. break the $100.00 bill and sent $80.00 back, thanking them for the gift and explaining that the agency has a $20.00 limit on gifts.

139. The BEST source for the rules, guidelines, and boundaries that define a professional relationship between a social worker and his/her client is:

a. an agency policy and procedure manual.
b. a handbook of clinical practice.
c. the *National Association of Social Workers (NASW) Code of Ethics.*
d. the social work credentialing board.

140. After a therapeutic relationship has ended, a client approaches a social worker to join in various family activities (birthday celebrations, holiday events, etc.). In light of the fact that a past professional relationship existed, yet acknowledging that it has formally ended, the social worker's BEST response would be to:

a. attend only small family gatherings as a show of care and support.
b. accept any invitation that time will allow to show uncompromising support.
c. attend some events, and invite the client out to others with them, so that the activities don't become one-sided.
d. cite the professional code of ethics, and clarify that even after a professional relationship ends, socializing is not permitted.

141. A client develops romantic feelings for his social worker, and repeatedly makes overtures and gestures indicating he would like to become involved. The BEST response would be for the social worker to:

a. refer the client to another professional promptly, emphasizing the need the client has to remain focused on resolving the important problems involved without any distraction.
b. talk about how much she wishes things were different, but cite the code of ethics as a barrier to becoming involved.
c. allow only a casually flirtatious relationship, making sure no legal boundaries are violated.
d. confront the client and demand that he/she stop behaving inappropriately.

142. If a client is to make a treatment-oriented decision, he/she must be fully informed about the purpose, risks, benefits, costs, and burdens that may be associated with the decision. The client may need to be educated about certain related features or issues in order to make a meaningful decision. While it may not be possible to foresee every eventuality, the client must receive all information that a "reasonable person" would expect in the given situation. This process of informing, educating, and reviewing prior to a treatment decision is called:

a. treatment orientation.
b. informed consent.
c. patient education.

legal disclosure.

143. The *NASW Code of Ethics* indicates that a client's ability to pay should be considered in setting fees. This means that a social worker may do all of the following EXCEPT:

a. decrease fees for a needy person already receiving services.
b. refer a potential to public programs prior beginning services.
c. liberally increase fees for a client who is particularly well off.
d. produce a sliding-scale fee rate that sets reasonable rates in advance.

144. An adult with an intellectual disability is in need of a medical procedure or treatment with a complex array of possible burdens and benefits with any choice that may be made. The client is able to understand many aspects of the procedure, and the immediate outcomes, but he/she may not be able to understand the full ramifications of future eventualities both with and without receiving the procedure or treatment. The best response would be to:

a. leave the client out of the decision-making process entirely.
b. turn the entire issue over to an ethics committee and don't remain involved.
c. tell the client just enough to make a decision that would be best.
d. involve the client in every aspect that he/she can properly understand, and allow his/her choices to govern where possible.

145. Social services may be paid for in numerous ways. The most obvious is by personal contribution (one pays for what they receive). All of the following are other ways that social services are funded, EXCEPT:

a. court ordered funding.
b. employer funded (direct pay).
c. government funded (i.e., direct pay or tax relief).
d. publicly funded (non-profit, public agencies).

146. The transfer of services once performed by the government to private entity providers is known as "privatization." Under these circumstances, the pay sources becomes:

a. the private institution that assumes the service provider role.
b. the government continues paying (but hopes the service will become cheaper to provide).
c. philanthropic organizations that can afford to pay.
d. personal contributions.

147. Housing assistance for those with low income is provided in all the following ways EXCEPT:

a. public housing (government built and owned housing offered at reduced rent rates.
b. subsidized housing ("Section 8" and other reduced rent and maintenance programs via government contributions).
c. home loan subsidy programs.
d. co-op housing (jointly owned via the renter and the government).

148. A source of food for low-income families is a federally-funded, state-administered program that provides purchase vouchers or coupons based on a family's size, income, and resources (e.g., a selective eligibility, means-tested program) that is known as:

a. S&H green stamps.
b. blue-book coupons.
c. food stamps.
d. nutrition voucher program.

149. A federally-funded, state-administered program providing food and assistance to pregnant women, mothers of children up to five months of age (if not breast feeding), breast-feeding mothers up to 12 months after delivery, and children up to five years of age is called the:

a. Women, Infants, and Children (WIC) program.
b. Women and Children Nutrition (WCN) program.
c. Women and Children Food (WCF) program.
d. Women and Children Health (WCH) program.

150. A locally funded program that provides delivery of food to low-income individuals who are unable to leave their home is called:

a. Food on the Move.
b. Meals on Wheels.
c. Drive and Dine.
d. Moveable Feast.

Answers and Explanations

1. B: The most appropriate diagnosis would be bulimia nervosa, severe. The diagnosis could not be anorexia nervosa, as she has not lost substantial weight and although of post-menarchal age, she has not experienced amenorrhea (much less for three consecutive cycles). The diagnosis is bulimia nervosa, as her behavior has persisted for three or more months. The degrees of severity are as follows: Mild: purging 1-3 times/week. Moderate: purging 4-7 times/week. Severe: purging 8-13 times/week. Extreme: purging 14 or more times/week.

2. A: The parent would be best served by joining an educational group. There are 7 major group types. Educational groups are formed to provide education, information, and essential skills. This parent needs to learn ways to manage medications, changing blood sugar, dietary needs, signs and symptoms of medical compromise, and so forth. An educational group is an ideal setting to learn how to provide optimum care and cope with inevitable changes and problems. A support group focuses on coping with a common problem (i.e., bereavement, etc.), but with less of an emphasis on learning and skill development. A self-help group is focused on behavioral change (i.e., alcoholics anonymous, etc.). A task group focuses on accomplishing a singular goal. Other group forms include: remedial groups (or psychotherapy groups, focused on personal growth, such as anger management), growth groups (developing personal potential), and socialization groups (to enhance interpersonal skills).

3. B: The most likely diagnosis is bipolar I, manic episode, with psychotic features, in full remission. Hypomania does not appear appropriate, as the client's behavior would likely have resulted in hospitalization had anyone been able to evaluate him during his period of mania. Cyclothymic disorder does not appear appropriate, as the client's conduct exceeded the threshold severity for hypomania, and no information is provided regarding depressive symptoms (though he may well have them). While there are some delusions likely involved in the episode described at the amusement park, there is no indication of hallucinations or disorganized speech, and it is better explained by the manic episode of a bipolar disorder given the other symptoms than by a brief psychotic episode (see criteria C of brief psychotic episode). Finally, the Bipolar I, manic episode is identified to be in full remission, as the client's manic symptoms appear to have completely resolved.

4. A: Bloom's taxonomy describes 3 types of learning:

- Cognitive: Learning and gaining intellectual skills and mastering categories of effective learning (knowledge, comprehension, application, analysis, synthesis, and evaluation).
- Affective: Recognizing categories of feelings and values from simple to complex (receiving and responding to phenomena, valuing, organizing, and internalizing values).
- Psychomotor: Mastering motor skills necessary for independence, following a progression from simple to complex (perception, set, guided response, mechanism, complex overt response, adaptation, and origination).

5. C: The incorrect cluster is Cluster B: Violent and/or Explosive Disorders (also referred to as "aggressive and intrusive conduct disorders"). These cluster descriptions have been provided by authors in various academic sources, although they only loosely describe each cluster's content. Cluster A includes: paranoid, schizoid, and schizotypal personality disorders. Cluster B includes: antisocial, borderline, histrionic, and narcissistic personality disorders. Finally Cluster C includes: Obsessive/Compulsive, Avoidant, and Dependent personality disorders. Clusters tend to run in families.

6. D: The "5 rights of delegation" include:

- Right task: The nurse determines an appropriate task to delegate for a specific patient.
- Right circumstance: The nurse has considered all relevant information to determine appropriateness of delegation.
- Right Person: The nurse chooses the right person based on education and skills to perform the task.
- Right direction: The nurse provides a clear description of the task, purpose, limits, and expected outcomes.
- Right supervision: The nurse must supervise, intervene as needed, and evaluate performance.

7. A: The most likely diagnosis for the young boy is attention deficit hyperactivity disorder (AD/HD). The term ADD is no longer in use, as it was excluded from a previous revision of the DSM. Conduct disorder would not be appropriate, as this child is not deliberately cruel or violent toward others. Obsessive compulsive disorder does not fit, as the child is not fixated on either ritualistic behavior or things, per se, but is simply chaotically busy. Oppositional defiant disorder is not an appropriate diagnosis, as this child is not deliberately uncooperative or argumentative. Caution is needed, however, in making the diagnosis. The behavior must not be situationally due to problems at home, and it must have persisted for six months or longer. Further, and most importantly, it must not be simple youthful exuberance or even a "high-energy" personality. Rather, the diagnosis is properly made when the behaviors are extreme, and well out of step with other peers. Having multiple involved adults complete the Connor Rating Scales (i.e., parents, grandparents, the teacher, a pediatrician, etc.) can reduce the chance of inappropriately applying this burdensome diagnosis.

8. C: While laziness, poor judgment, and inadequate supervision may all be factors, failing to provide reasonable care based upon usual and customary standards and expertise is an example of negligent conduct. Reasonable care uses rationale for decision-making in relation to providing care. Gross negligence is willfully providing inadequate care while disregarding the safety and security of another. Contributory negligence involves the injured party contributing to his/her own harm. Comparative negligence assigns a percentage amount of negligence to each individual involved.

9. B: The social worker's practice framework may vary depending upon the issues involved, resources, etc., and thus multiple practice frameworks may be required to properly serve the needs of an agency and its clients. The practice framework is based upon time and resources available, treatment modality required, the issue to be addressed, the outcomes sought, and an appropriate theoretical framework.

10. B: This is an example of a natural group. The group occurred naturally, and pre-existed the presence of the social worker. Some concern exists in formal settings, such as a hospital, when natural groups form. A primary concern is when misinformation emerges and is perpetuated via the group. Therefore, it may become necessary for the group to be formalized. In this situation an open group structure (that allows members to join and leave as they desire) may be advantageous. A closed group typically has set meeting times and an end-date (10 weeks, etc.), fosters greater intimacy and group cohesion, and allows for graduated information and teaching. It will of necessity be a short-term structure, as pediatric patients will ultimately be discharged. Formed groups are intentionally arranged, such as a court-ordered group for drug offenders.

11. A: An ecosystems framework framework is largely derived from Ecological Systems Theory (also called "Development in Context" or "Human Ecology" theory). It addresses five environmental systems, and assumes bi-directional influences within and between the systems. Developed by Urie

Bronfenbrenner, a developmental psychologist, the five systems are: 1) the Microsystem (family, peers, neighborhood, and other social environments; 2) the Mesosystem (the connections between these environments; 3) the Exosystem (settings which indirectly affect development, such as parental work); 4) the Macrosystem (the cultural context); and 5) the Chronosystem (events and transitions over the life course). Biology is also relevant, thus the theory is sometimes called the "Bio-Ecological Systems Theory." The roles, norms, and rules of each system shape psychological development throughout life.

12. D: Both the patient's verbal and non-verbal responses may be of equal importance. Patients may look away or become tense if they are not telling the truth or don't want to answer. Thus, information elicited during an interview should include not only the patient's factual responses but also attitudes and concerns. Nurses should ask open-ended information questions rather than yes/no questions, and should follow-up with clarifying questions. Providing a list of options and rephrasing a patient's statement may encourage the patient to provide more information.

13. D: This is called a feminist framework. Although largely used only when working with female clients, the framework can be extended to male clients, especially when the presenting problem involves sex role issues, stereotypic expectations, and/or reverse role gender discrimination (female on male).

14. A: Mentoring is providing professional guidance, as well as being someone to whom a staff person can bring questions or concerns. Role modeling takes place when one nurse serves as a role for others, such as demonstrating those behaviors and responses that advocate for the patient and show care. Supervising is ensuring that delegated tasks and duties are done correctly. Coaching involves providing staff with tools and ways to respond, or procedures to follow, to help staff become more effective.

15. C: This is a description of an ethnic-sensitive framework. Broadly construing this framework to include any and all major elements that a client uses to define and identify the self (work, external affiliations, historical context, etc.), will allow this framework to be most effective. Thus, a retired military man who identifies strongly with his status as a past prisoner of war during a particular military era (e.g., a Vietnam veteran, prisoner of war, career soldier, etc.) would benefit from a practice approach that is sensitive to and acknowledges this background in the client's life, relationships, and psychological makeup.

16. D: Behavior modification and compliance rates are the best determinants of the effectiveness of patient education. Patients may be satisfied, may understand, and may be able to provide a demonstration, but if they don't utilize what they have learned the education has not been effective for that patient. Behavior modification involves thorough observation and measurement, identifying behavior that needs to be changed and then planning and instituting interventions. Compliance rates should be determined by observation at necessary intervals and on multiple occasions.

17. B: The psychoanalytic approach views behavior as derived from unconscious drives and motivations, views disorders and dysfunction as emerging from internal conflicts and anxiety, and seeks to facilitate the conscious awareness of previously repressed information. This approach is built upon the concepts and theory of Sigmund Freud and others who have followed him. The approach is also sometimes called a "psychodynamic" approach.

18. B: The right to pain control is part of the Patients' Bill of Rights. Affordable healthcare and access to latest medical technology are not included. The right to sue is not directly included, but

patients are entitled to a procedure for registering complaints or grievances. Other provisions include respect for patient, informed consent, advance directives, and end of life care, privacy and confidentiality, protection from abuse and neglect, protection during research, appraisal of outcomes, appeal procedures, an organizational code of ethical behaviors, and procedures for donating and procuring organs/tissues.

19. C: Transference (client to social worker) and countertransference (social worker to client) include emotions, reactions, defenses, desires, and feelings that come to bear on the relationship and/or the problem, whether consciously or unconsciously.

20. B: This should notify the social worker to focus attention on the issue of Jamie's mother. Even when a client is verbal and appears to be invested in honestly exploring significant issues, there often is some resistance to confronting the most pertinent (and painful) issues. Jamie's behavior is indicative of this type of situation.

21. A: The phases of treatment, as specific to psychoanalysis, include the elements of engagement (building rapport, trust, etc.), contracting (identifying goals and responsibilities), treatment processes, and termination (reviewing goals achieved and ways to independently further progress).

22. D: Recruiting membership to ensure a large and diverse population, ideally consisting of more than 20 group members, is NOT integral in effective group leadership. Most theorists indicate that effective groups should not have memberships exceeding 8-12. The younger the group membership, the smaller the ideal group (preteens: 3-4; teens: 6-8; young adults: 8-10).

23. C: The behavioral approach, sometimes also simply called "behavior modification," believes that as long as a problem can be "operationally defined" (in terms of the specific change needed and the consequences necessary to induce change) virtually every problem can be resolved by resorting to behavioral modification techniques. This approach is most effective when the client voluntarily undertakes treatment, but involuntary treatment can also be successful if proper reinforcements and/or consequences can be integrated into the change process. This approach is based on principles of social learning theory, operant conditioning, behavioral theory, and classical (respondent) conditioning theory.

24. C: The legal document that designates someone to make decisions regarding medical and end-of-life care if a patient is mentally incompetent is a Durable Power of Attorney for Health Care. This is one type of Advance Directive, which can also include a living will, a medical power of attorney, and other specific requests of the patient regarding his or her health care. A Do-Not-Resuscitate order is a physician-generated document that is completed when a patient does not want resuscitative treatment in an end-of-life situation. A General Power of Attorney allows a designated person to make decisions for a person over broader areas, including financial concerns.

25. D: In the cognitive approach, considerable work must be done to seek out and clarify a client's false beliefs and misconceptions that underlie problem behaviors and interpersonal issues. This approach has a significant educational component, as the client must be taught ways to identify these errant thoughts and how to circumvent and/or overcome them using new strategies and coping skills.

26. B: Specifying the group's objectives. All other tasks can only be successfully pursued once the group's goals and objectives have been clarified. The other options presented could actually be addressed and incorporated or dismissed during the goal and objective clarification process.

27. B: Psychoanalysis utilizes treatment concepts and techniques such as dream analysis, exploration of the past, free association, ventilation, sustainment, confrontation and direct influence.

28. B: Jung proposed the theory of individualism. He theorized that one's personality continued to develop over the lifespan. Personality comprises ego, personal unconsciousness, and collective unconsciousness. Personality can be introverted or extroverted, but a balance is necessary for emotional health. Jung theorized that during middle age, people begin to question their values, beliefs, and attainments. As they continue to age, they turn more inward. Successful aging is when people value themselves more than the concern they have for external things, losses, and physical limitations.

29. A: Behavioral therapy was formulated by John Watson and Ivan Pavlov (classical conditioning) and B.F. Skinner (operant conditioning). Additional social worker work is done in analyzing client tally sheets, charts, journal entries, etc., in search of patterns and insights that would assist in refining key insights in to behavioral antecedents, and improving selected reinforcers and consequences. Collateral work must also be done regarding client- social worker contract revision and consequences for contract agreement violation, etc.

30. C: This is characteristic of Stage 4: Differentiation. During this stage, group members display opinions and differing views more readily. Stage 1, pre-affiliation, involves getting acquainted and group appraisal. Stage 2, power and control, involves the development of roles and leadership within the group. Stage 3, intimacy, refers to the development of group cohesion and solidarity. Stage 5, separation, involves preparation for termination, including goal review, anticipated loss, and closure.

31. C: Cognitive therapy utilizes treatment concepts and techniques such as clarification, explanation, interpretation, paradoxical direction, reflection, and writing.

32. A: Group instruction is more cost effective than one-on-one instruction because a number of patients/family can be served at one time. Group presentations are usually more rigidly scripted and scheduled for a particular time period, so family and patients have less control. Questions may be more limited, but group instruction also allows patients/families with similar concerns to interact. Group instruction is particularly useful for general types of instruction, such as managing diet or other lifestyle issues.

33. D: Gestalt therapy, founded by Frederick and Laura Perls, in the 1940s, teaches a phenomenological method of awareness, with a focus on immediate perceptions, feelings, and actions as separate from interpreting and recapitulating preexisting attitudes. In this approach, explanations and interpretations are set aside in favor of what is directly perceived and felt.

34. B: The social worker should self-examine to determine possible reasons for the reaction. While it may be prudent for a social worker to speak with a supervisor or colleague about what he or she is experiencing, the best first step would be self-examination. Self-awareness is an important quality in a competent social worker, which is why social workers often are urged to enter counseling themselves. It's important for a social worker to be self-aware in order to competently treat clients.

35. B: These are characteristics of task-centered therapy. It is important to note that, because this form of therapy is client-driven, with the social worker only assisting by means of facilitation, individuals who are not committed to change would not be good candidates for this form of

therapy. It is generally short-term (6-12 sessions), and involves open sharing between both the client and the social worker (i.e., no "hidden agendas").

36. D: Pain Assessment in Advanced Dementia (PAINAD) scale utilizes careful observation of non-verbal behavior to evaluate pain, noting changes in:

- Respirations: Rapid, labored, with short periods of hyperventilation or Cheyne-stokes.
- Vocalization: Negative or absent speech, moaning, and crying out as pain increases.
- Facial expression: Sad, frightened, frowning, grimacing.
- Body language: Tense, fidgeting, pacing, clenching fists, and lying in a fetal position as pain increases.
- Consolability: Less easily distractible or consolable as pain increases.

37. C: Gestalt therapy utilizes treatment concepts and techniques such as dialogue, enactment of dreams, exaggeration, exposure of the obvious, and rehearsal to overcome barriers such as confluence, introjection, projection and retroflection.

38. A: The Confusion Assessment Method is used to assess the development of delirium and is intended for use by those without psychiatric training. The assessment tool covers 9 factors:

- Onset: Acute changes in mental status.
- Attention: Inattentive, stable, or fluctuating.
- Thinking: Disorganized, rambling, switching topics, illogical.
- Level of consciousness: Altered (ranging from alert to coma).
- Orientation: Time, place, person.
- Memory: Impaired.
- Perceptual disturbances: Hallucinations, illusions.
- Psychomotor abnormalities: Agitations or retardation.
- Sleep-wake cycle: Awake at night, sleepy in the daytime.

39. D: The crisis intervention approach sees periods of intense trauma as optimal for effecting change, and seeks to equip clients with new and/or more effective coping skills to manage traumatic situation. The goal is not to produce a "cure" but to help clients more adequately cope until the worst of the crisis has passed. Once the crisis has passed, the client may well be in need of further psychotherapeutic intervention.

40. D: Most likely, counseling will become interminable. Counseling can be interminable when factors exist that limit its ability to be effective. One of those factors is when therapy goals are unrealistic. In this case, the goal of never experiencing conflict when making decisions is an unrealistic one, so counseling is likely to be interminable unless the error is noted and corrected.

41. A: Family therapy views family as composed of multiple subsystems and holds views that the dysfunction and conflict in any one subsystem can penetrate and affect the other subsystems. This form of therapy is based largely upon systems theory and communication theory.

42. A: A problem list focuses on a prioritized list of patient problems based on assessment data, history, and interview. Trying to deal with all patient problems without prioritizing them to determine which are the most critical can result in ineffective care. Patients are not always aware of their own needs regarding health care or intervention, and standardized lists of problems may be used as a guide but will not always match the individual's circumstances.

43. A: Group therapy arises from the belief that individuals in similar situations can identify with, comfort, reassure and help one another. It is important to note, however, that group therapy is typically an adjunctive approach (sometimes called a "complementary therapy" or "complementary intervention"), rather than an individual's only source of treatment. The seven major types of groups are: 1) educational groups; 2) growth groups (consciousness raising); 3) remedial groups (or "psychotherapy groups" where issues, such as anger, are encountered); 4) self-help groups (such as Alcoholics Anonymous); 5) socialization groups (to improve interpersonal skills); 6) support groups (or "mutual sharing groups" for those with common concerns, such as bereavement); and 7) task groups (focused on achieving specific goals, such as job location, etc.).

44. B: Advocacy is working for the best interests of the patient despite conflicting personal and assisting patients to have access to appropriate resources. Moral agency is the ability to recognize needs and a willingness take action to influence the wholesome outcome of a conflict or decision. Agency is a general willingness to act arising from openness and the recognition of involved issues. Collaboration is working together to achieve better results.

45. C: These are all stages of group development. During these stages, the social worker needs to: 1) facilitate familiarity and elicit participation; 2) clarify roles; 3) develop group cohesion; 4) support individual differences; and 5) foster independence. The use of a "Sociogram" (a chart or diagram depicting group member relationships) can aid the social worker in revealing, monitoring, and intervening (if necessary) in group member interactions and bonding.

46. D: Biofeedback uses monitoring devices to allow people to control their own physiological responses. People use information (feedback) from ECG, EMG, EEG, galvanic skin response, pulse, BP, and temperature to differentiate between the abnormal and the desired state. People with hypertension will use the feedback about their BP to help them lower it by relaxing, deep breathing, or other activities. The monitoring devices show when their efforts are effective. Biofeedback may be used to control heart rate, BP, pain, incontinence, and muscle strength.

47. B: Crisis intervention utilizes treatment concepts largely oriented around immediate problem-solving, stress reduction, coping skill enhancement, support system building, and emotional buffering. Because engagement is during a crisis experience, and is typically short-term in nature, the focus is less on assessment than on buffering, support system building, stress reduction, etc.

48. A: The social worker should take a position of extreme caution. Suicidal clients who suddenly feel better are often not improving but rather are less conflicted because they have made the decision to take their lives. This is when extreme caution should be exercised by the social worker, because the risk to the client is actually higher.

49. D: These treatment approaches are associated with family therapy. This modality also uses the "strategic family therapy approach," which focuses on the function of family rules and behavior patterns. The goal of the social worker is to devise interventions which will elicit functional behavioral patterns, and revise those family rules which defeat or impede appropriate family relationships and conduct.

50. C: Transference is likely causing these client's feelings. Transference is a Freudian term that describes a client's placing feelings for another onto the social worker. In this case, especially because of the problematic relationship issues, the client is likely to be transferring feelings inaccurately onto the social worker.

51. C: Forced groups are not a type of group therapy structure. While some groups are formed of members under court order, there is no such group category, nor would a group, itself, seek to force attendance.

52. A: The best approach to solving a problem that involves 3 different departments is to form an interdisciplinary team of representative participants to work together and find a solution. This allows all parties to have a voice and to work toward compromise, while avoiding the confusion caused by too many competing interests. If administration makes a decision independently, or picks one of the proposed solutions over another, all or many staff members may feel their voices weren't heard. Trying to gather all members of 3 departments together for brainstorming is usually impractical, and an unnecessary use of employee time and resources.

53. B: This is the therapeutic modality of the crisis intervention approach. Interventions tend to be problem-solving and short-term in nature, in keeping with the concept of a crisis. The social worker must have sufficient expertise in the crisis issue (grief, suicide, rape, etc.) to be effective, but must also use caution to not foster dependency in the relationship with the client, who may be sufficiently overwhelmed as to be uncharacteristically needy.

54. A: A social worker may limit the client's right to self-determination when there's a threat to self or others. Social workers are expected to respect a client's right to self-determination. However, if a client's choice of action threatens himself or the welfare of others, a social worker may limit that right.

55. B. Individuals typically pass through five stages of grief to reconcile a loss (Kübler-Ross, 1969):

1. *Denial*, a defense mechanism that protects an individual from the full initial impact of the loss.
2. *Anger*, at the irretrievability of the loss.
3. *Bargaining*, considering all "what if" and "if only" elements that could have prevented or could restore (appeals to God, etc.) the loss.
4. *Despair/depression*, as the full meaning of the loss emerges.
5. *Acceptance*, surrendering to loss and coming to believe in eventual recovery.

56. A: The best readability level is grade 6. The average American reads effectively at the 6th to 8th grade level (regardless of education achieved), and research shows that even people with much higher reading skills learn medical and health information most effectively when the material is presented at the 6th to 8th grade readability level. A grade 3 level would be too simplified for most native speakers of English, but might be appropriate for immigrant populations with limited English.

57. D: Systems theory. The systems may be "open" (accepting of outside input) or "closed" (resisting outside forces and input). Working with a system from a "horizontal approach" is to limit the scope of intervention to a specific community and those things occurring within it. In contrast, a "vertical approach" reaches well beyond the identified community, extending, for example, to policies, programs, and resources outside the community that can be brought to bear in addressing community concerns.

58. D: Piaget's stages of cognitive development relate to changes in cognitive abilities related to age and development, and the "formal operational" stage is characterized by logical thinking and the use of abstraction:

- Sensorimotor (0 – 2): Infants learn about cause and effect and the permanence of objects.
- Preoperational (2 – 7): Thinking is concrete and tangible at the preconceptual stage, and later becomes intuitive. These children are egocentric.
- Concrete operational (7 – 11): Children develop the concept of conservation and reasoning becomes inductive.
- Formal operational (11 – 15): Adolescents develop the ability to use abstract thought and to develop and test hypotheses.

59. B: The ecosystems theory (also called the "Life Model Theory) focuses on the relationship between living things and their environment, sees "adaptation" as the process by which individuals and the environment accommodate each other, and views dysfunction as a failure to cooperate and accommodate. In direct practice, social workers use ecosystems theory to help clients recognize the demands of their environment and then better accommodate. In community practice, social workers use ecosystems theory to pursue community, policy, and program change in ways to make the environment more receptive to the individual.

60. C: Autocratic leaders make decisions independently and strictly enforce rules. Bureaucratic leaders follow organizational rules exactly and expect others to do so, as well. Laissez-faire leaders exert little direct control and allow others to make decisions with little interference. Participatory leaders present a potential decision and make a final decision based on input from team members. Consultative leaders present a decision and welcome input, but rarely change their decisions. Democratic leaders present a problem and ask the team to arrive at a solution, although these leaders make the final decision.

61. C: In Gestalt theory, great attention is given to the immediate therapeutic encounter as an "experience" from which to gain awareness and increased understanding of the "here and now," which is considered to be a more reliable source of understanding than processes of cognitive interpretation.

62. A: Non-verbal communication includes:

- Eye contact: Eye contact shows connection. Avoidance may indicate fear, distrust, lack of truthfulness, or (in some cultures) respect.
- Tone: A high-pitched vocal tone may indicate nervousness or stress.
- Touch: People may touch themselves (picking, lip-licking, rubbing their hands together, etc.) if they are anxious.
- Gestures: Tapping of the foot or fidgeting may indicate nervousness. The hands may be used to emphasize meaning.
- Posture: Slumping may indicate lack of interest or withdrawal.

63. D: Psychosocial therapy (also referred to as "bio-psycho-social therapy") focuses on the multidimensional aspects of the individual and engages the client in the context of his/her personal history, strengths, weaknesses, resources, wants and needs. The earliest proponent of this form of therapy was Florence Hollis (1963), who was later joined by Mary Woods (who continued this work after Hollis' death).

64. B: The social worker should consult with a social worker trained in psychosis. A social worker is ethically responsible to practice only within those areas where he or she is competent. Because the client's welfare must be paramount, the social worker in this case should not discontinue counseling but should consult with someone who is competent in psychosis and proceed from there.

65. A: Solution-focused therapy sees clients as competent to co-construct goals and strategies and as experts regarding their own lives and experiences. It encourages change by doing something differently, even while recognizing the only small steps need to be taken, and suggests that "if it isn't broken, don't fix it" and that "if it didn't work, try something different." It originated at the Brief Family Therapy Center (BFTC) in Milwaukee, and Steve de Shazer was one of the primary originators.

66. B: Selye's biological theory of stress and aging states that stress is a body response to demands requiring positive or negative adaptation, characterized by the "generalized adaptation syndrome," which includes 3 stages:

- Alarm: Fight or flight response.
- Resistance: The body mobilizes to resist a threat, focusing on those organs most involved in an adaptive response.
- Exhaustion: As the body is weakened and overwhelmed, organs/systems begin to deteriorate (hypertrophy/atrophy) and can no longer cope with stress, resulting in stress-related illnesses and eventual death.

67. B: Logotherapy is used primarily with the elderly and with those experiencing loss. It is often adjunctive to other therapeutic interventions that focus on important survivor questions and that see three key paths to meaning. The originator of this therapeutic approach was Viktor Emil Frankl (author of the best-selling book "Man's Search for Meaning").

68. C: Yes, under all circumstances this presents a concern This situation may present a dual relationship that can create a conflict of interest. Conflicts of interest are not ethically allowed in counseling relationships and are to be avoided.

69. D: Transactional analysis (TA) is based on fundamental units of social intercourse and fundamental units of social action. The founder of this theory was Eric Berne, who developed it during the 1950s. Transactional Analysis is the method for studying interactions between individuals. Departing from the Freudian dialogue approach, TA social workers simply observe communication processes (words, body language, facial expressions), often in group settings, to explore a client's transactions – in light of the fact that complete communication importance is: actual word - 7%; word delivery style (tone, inflections, etc.) - 38%; and facial expressions - 55%. Through such analyses, interactive styles can be identified, and changes made (where needed) to enhance an individual's interpersonal strengths and ultimate successes.

70. A: The social worker must give care to discussing the limits of confidentiality. Confidentiality is a critical issue in social work, but there are limits, and a client should be made aware of those limits. In this case, suicide ideation may present a situation where confidentiality needs to be breached. To ensure a positive client/ social worker relationship, the client should be made particularly aware of confidentiality limits.

71. C: These two forms of conditioning, in order, are classical conditioning and operant conditioning. Stimuli that induce a reaction without training are called "primary" or

"unconditioned" stimuli (US). They include food, pain, and other "hardwired" or "instinctive" stimuli. Stimuli that do not induce a desire reaction until after conditioning has occurred are called secondary or conditioned stimuli.

72. B: The social worker should provide the records and help to interpret them. Social workers have a responsibility to provide clients with their records upon request. In some cases, however, interpretation may be needed. Also, social workers should be careful that the confidentiality of other people's material in an individual's records is protected.

73. D: The client would be considered not in remission, due to not meeting timeframe for remission. Early remission starts at 3 months and continues to 12 months of symptom free except craving. Sustained remission is 12 months or more symptom free, except craving. The client has only been free from substance use for 10 weeks, so he doesn't meet either of those criteria yet. When the client reaches 3 months, even if he is using a maintenance therapy medication he can be considered in remission, it will just be noted "on maintenance therapy". For the rest of the client's life he may experience craving, but as long as he does not have any other symptoms he will still be considered "in remission."

74. A: A correlation coefficient of 1.0 indicates a perfect relationship between two variables.

75. D: The social worker should refer the client to another social worker. It is not considered ethically responsible to enter into a counseling relationship with someone with whom the social worker previously had a sexual relationship. Professional boundaries are difficult to maintain in this situation, and harm to the client could ensue.

76. B: The social worker should thoughtfully but explicitly address and explore the behavior. Ignoring the behavior offers the couple no opportunity to address and overcome it. Mentioning the behavior only casually allows it to be equally casually dismissed. Confronting a couple who is in pain from a profound loss and already in fragile state could be perceived as overly aggressive, potentially leading to diminished rapport and/or therapeutic estrangement.

77. D: Sources where substances were obtained are not a necessary part of the assessment process. There is no reporting requirement for this, and it is not germane to the treatment process.

78. D: A statistical test is comprised of a research hypothesis, a null hypothesis, a test statistic, a rejection region and a conclusion. The research hypothesis is symbolized as "H_A," the null hypothesis is symbolized as "H_O," the test statistic is symbolized as "TS," and the rejection region is symbolized as "RR."

79. C: Drug "affinity" testing to determine the level of addiction present is not a treatment modality for substance abuse. There is no laboratory test to determine an individual's level of addiction – particularly because much of the addictive experience is psychological and not just physiological.

80. B: Simply asking the client directly why he/she is unwilling to cooperate would be the least effective approach in overcoming the client's reluctance. The direct approach is sometimes ideal. However, asking a why question can be particularly problematic in a situation of resistance because the client may feel that he/she is being judged or challenged in his response. The question itself suggests some belligerence or non-cooperation on the part of the client, and it can produce a confrontational situation that could damage the working relationship. Often asking a client to "tell me more about that" serves the same purpose, without the potential for disrupting the relationship.

81. B: Generally, deep seated issues (the focus of psychoanalytic therapy) are not dealt with in a substance abuse treatment program. Most focus on very practical strategies for increasing awareness and breaking the cycle of substance abuse relapse (changing peers, changing areas, becoming more productive and attentive to life, improving home relationships, etc.). Because most addictions are chronic in nature, individuals require long-term interventions. Cost and efficacy issues generally move individuals into long-term self-help resources, such as Alcoholics Anonymous and Narcotics Anonymous, etc.

82. A: Alpha value refers to the threshold necessary to decide whether an intervention produced an outcome, or whether it was the result of a chance "statistical significance."

83. B: According to studies, 90 days (three months) is the minimum period in a residential treatment program if the likelihood of an enhanced long-term outcome is to be achieved.

84. A: The social worker's best response is to aid the client in exploring his difficulties in this area. It would be helpful to the client to explore his reluctance further, certainly in deference to his capacity to work well in other opposite-gender relationships. If the client remains entirely unwilling to address the issue, or if subsequent exploration does not resolve the client's concerns, then a case transfer or referral out would be most appropriate.

85. D: Cocaine is classified as a stimulant. In 1914, with the Harrison Drug Act, cocaine was erroneously classified, in the eyes of the law, as a narcotic. This legal designation has never been revised, thus, identifying it as a narcotic would be "legally" correct. However, pharmaceutically and psychoactively, cocaine is a stimulant; thus, this would be the most correct answer, from an abuse and rehabilitation perspective.

86. B: Means tested programs is not a category of social service programs. Universal programs are open to everyone, without any exclusion criteria. Exceptional eligibility programs are only available to certain groups with common needs, such as the Veteran's Health Administration. Selective eligibility programs are either "means tested" (including asset evaluation) or "income-tested" (looking solely at financial income).

87. C: Most anxiolytics (anti-anxiety medications) are benzodiazepines, which makes them depressants in their action on the central nervous system. There are exceptions, however, such as buspirone (BuSpar), which is a psychotropic drug that is a serotonin receptor stimulant.

88. C: Interdisciplinary palliative care teams ensure that providers from multiple specialties (e.g., physician, social worker, nurse, chaplain) can collaborate with the patient and family to craft a care plan that meets the needs and goals of the patient. Care is directed primarily by the patient. Ideally, the team provides information and elicits patient values, preferences, and goals as they pertain to end-of-life care. Once this is completed, specific challenges can be identified and possible solutions planned. Interventions are then provided to the patient and family in accordance with the formulated plan. Reassessments and changes in the care plan are made as illness progresses or preferences or goals change.

89. D: All of the above. Communication, from the perspective of social work, must be broadly defined, as all forms of communication will be important in a therapeutic context. It encompasses verbal expressions between two or more individuals, body language conveying meaning between two or more individuals and written expressions shared between two or more individuals.

90. C: To be eligible to receive social security retirement benefits, an individual must have earned a lifetime credit total of 40 credits. For those born before 1960, the retirement age for maximum benefits is 65. For those born in or after 1960, the age is 67.

91. A: While the client's grooming and hygiene may indicate a great deal about the client and his or her habits, financial status, mental and physical health, etc., these factors should not have direct influence on the communication experience.

92. D: Jehovah's Witnesses do not allow transfusions of blood or blood products. Some may allow auto-transfusion for blood loss.

93. C: The social worker should discuss with him the difficulty he is experiencing, and encourage him to take more time. "Sentence finishing" often substitutes the social worker's thoughts in place of the clients, which the client may then accept to relieve the burden he is feeling. Pressing the client to continue will often make the problem worse. Ignoring the problem and waiting indefinitely may lead to premature termination.

94. D: This program is administered by the Social Security Administration, where the program is referred to as Social Security Disability (SSD).

95. B: The social worker would revise the meeting to cover only very basic issues until better arrangements can be made. Abruptly terminating a meeting may leave the client feeling rejected and upset after the efforts made to attend. Delaying the meeting can cause similar problems. Resorting to the use of one's limited language skills could lead to misunderstandings and unnecessary confusion. Therefore, revising the meeting to pursue only basic information intake and to establish simple rapport would be advantageous.

96. B: The first step should be to acknowledge the highly ambivalent feelings she is experiencing. There is a natural tendency is to hasten and point out the classic features of relationship abuse. However, this approach is likely to immediately alienate the client. Importantly, she has already expressed ambivalent feelings. Allowing her to process those feelings, and then moving on to exploring other past relationships, and eventually reality-testing this one is typically much more successful approach.

97. D: Asking "why" questions can be problematic because the client may feel judged or challenged in his response. While many other problems may emerge from "why" questions, a sense of being judged is perhaps the most significant among them. Often asking a client to "tell me more about that" serves the same purpose, without the potential for disrupting the relationship.

98. C: A social insurance program for individuals sustaining employment-related injuries is the Worker's Compensation Program. To be eligible, the injuries sustained must not have occurred through gross negligence, willful misconduct, or intoxication.

99. A: The word "okay" is often taken to mean, "I understand now, there's no need to continue." Thus, other responses would be more likely to cause the client to continue sharing.

100. C: In this situation, the social worker should use reflective listening techniques and allow the client more time. Aggressive and/or confrontational techniques are unlikely to induce change in a client with a predisposition to defer to others. It becomes necessary to more skillfully apply reflective listening techniques to bring this client out. This will require the social worker to be more tolerant of a slower therapeutic pace, and carefully guard against completing the client's sentences to overcome awkward pauses and periods of silence.

101. C: Rephrasing is used to emphasize what the client said, while paraphrasing is used to show mutual understanding. Rephrasing changes only a few words that further emphasize what the client has said (e.g. "the surgery hurt" to "so, the surgery was very painful"). Paraphrasing, however, is virtually an unchanged restatement of the client's words to demonstrate that she was heard.

102. B: The Supplemental Security Income program supports individuals falling below the "poverty line" threshold, including the working poor and individuals who are elderly, disabled and/or blind.

103. B: Substitution is not an element of active listening. Telling a client what oneself would do not only turns the conversation away from him and his own thinking, but it closes off further communication as the authority figure "has spoken" and seemingly concluded that scenario.

104. C. Symbols of alcohol misuse include:

- Confusion/Disorientation
- Loss of motor control
- Convulsions
- Shock
- Shallow respiration
- Involuntary defecation
- Drowsiness
- Respiratory depression
- Possible death

105. B: "Could you tell me more about..." is an open-ended, non-leading question that encourages the client to continue and to share more.

106. C: The Temporary Assistance for Needy Families (TANF) program was renamed in 1966, stemming from the "Aid for Families with Dependent Children" program. It was revised to be a transitional program from welfare to work.

107. A: A stacked or complex question contains multiple parts, potentially leaving a client confused or unclear what the question was, or at least uncertain which part to answer first. For example, "Was the part that you didn't understand where he told you to stop, or where he asked for your supervisor, or where he said that you could be liable for that?" This question can easily leave a client confused and uncertain how to respond. Feelings such as this can make the client less willing to communicate.

108. A. Prozac is an SSRI used to treat depression. Medications used to treat the psychotic symptoms of schizophrenia include:

Old antipsychotics:

- Haldol (haloperidol)
- Thorazine (chlorpromazine)
- Mellaril (thioridazine)
- Stelazine (trifluoperazine)
- Prolixin (Fluphenazine)
- Navane (thiothixene)
- Clozaril (clozapine)

Newer or atypical antipsychotics:

- Clozaril
- Risperdal
- Seroquel
- Zyprexa (olanzapine)
- Abilify

109. D: Partialization is the process of breaking down the concerns at hand into smaller, more manageable parts. For example, "Well, if we take these things one at a time, maybe we can start with..."

110. A: Two components of the federal health insurance program for the elderly (Medicare) are medical insurance and hospital insurance. The hospitalization coverage portion is known as Medicare Part A, and the medical care coverage portion is known as Medicare Part B. Expansions in recent years have also resulted in Medicare Part C (a combined A & B program administered by private health insurance companies, HMOs, etc.), and Medicare Part D (prescription drug coverage).

111. C: The relationship between a social worker and a client should be characterized as a professional relationship, which is necessary for an effective bond of trust, and to facilitate essential disclosure necessary to achieve change.

112. D: Meals on Wheels is a locally funded program, not a federally funded program. Federally funded programs include the Elderly Nutrition Program, the Food Stamps Programs, and the Women, Infants and Children (WIC) program.

113. B: The social worker does not assume the role of enforcer and regulator. Quality social work is all about providing insights and options. It is not about punitive accountability, enforcement, or policing. Assuming such roles will extinguish the trust and sustaining power of the therapeutic relationship that must predominate. While social workers may be called upon to provide protective roles in investigating abuse, the law enforcement and the criminal justice system will mete out the necessary consequences, not social work staff, who must still refrain from caustic critique and recrimination.

114. C: The "Id" would be the part of the personality driving the behavior of a serial rapist. It is the most primitive part of the personality, and the libido is its most basic instinctual drive. The "Ego" is more rational, and mediates between individual wants and environmental demands. As the Ego develops, the "Reality Principle" arises, introducing compromise. The "Superego" incorporates ethical and moral constraints on behavior. It is composed of two parts: 1) the "Conscience" (i.e., the "do not do" behaviors); and 2) the "Ego Ideal" (regulating the "should do" behaviors). Development should be complete by about age five, per Freud.

115 D: The NASW social work primary mission is dedicated to meeting basic human needs and enhancing human well-being from a social context, including societal environmental forces that bear on problems in everyday life.

116. B: These are the psychosexual stages of development. The oral stage represents that period when oral gratification is a primary source of fulfillment (from 0-18 months of age). The anal stage refers to the shift of attention to bowel control as a source of accomplishment (18 months to three years). The phallic stage refers to the shift of attention from anus to genitals (3-6 years of age). The latency stage refers to the period of accommodation of sexual urges into socially acceptable

behaviors (6-12 years of age). Finally, the genital stage (from 12 to adulthood) marks the maturing of genital interest into a proper adult role and feelings.

117. A: Social work's core values include competence, individual dignity, integrity, quality human relationships, service and social justice.

118. D: Erikson called these two opposing features dystonic and syntonic. Taking Stage 1 (trust vs. distrust) as an example, one may be naturally trusting or naturally distrusting. Regardless, one part of this stage "syntonic" (in natural accord with one's personality) and one part will be "dystonic" (not easily accommodated in one's natural personality). The "crisis" is coming to terms with both. One must learn to be appropriately trusting in key situations in order to have fulfilling and meaningful relationships. Yet one must not become so trusting as to be vulnerable to abuse in situations that should not involve immediate trust. Upon resolving this dichotomy, one will be prepared to move on to the next developmental stage.

119. C: The social worker is a mandated reporter. This includes even reasonable suspicions of abuse – a client who is routinely dressed improperly for the weather, has bruises, is malnourished, is abandoned alone when supervision is needed, etc. – must all be reported, along with frank evidence of abuse.

120. C: Hartmann proposed that the ego has eight functions. The eight functions of the Ego are:

- Reality testing
- Impulse control
- Affect regulation
- Judgment
- Object relations
- Thought processes
- Defensive functioning
- Synthesis

121. B: The primary form of abuse to be suspected here is financial abuse. This is also a form of abuse that must be reported and investigated by the proper authorities.

122. B: Hartmann believed the Id and the Ego to be rudimentarily present from birth forward, therefore in all children. He also believed that the Ego has the capacity to function independently, while Freud saw the Ego functioning as a mediator (with the Id) and receiving mediation through the Superego.

123. D: The social worker's duty now is to contact the client's wife to inform her of the danger. According to recent interpretations of the Tarasoff v. Regents of the University of California case (1976, California Supreme Court ruling) confidentiality, in this situation, may be breeched if: 1) the HIV infection is known; 2) unprotected sex (or sharing of needles) is occurring; 3) the behavior is actually unsafe; 4) the client refuses to modify his behavior even after being counseled regarding the harm; and 5) if HIV transmission will likely occur.

124. D: This theory is called the Object Relations Theory. Derived both from Freud's Psychoanalytic Theory and Hartmann's Ego Psychology, it focuses on Ego organization during the first 3½ years of life, when differentiation between self and others is emerging.

125. C: Publication in a reputable professional journal is not an exception for consent. Regardless of the compelling nature of the information, or the good it might do others, records cannot be released

for publication without consent from the individual. While PL 93-579 applies only to federal agencies and settings, virtually all state and local government agencies have promulgated these same practices.

126. C: Splitting serves to repress, disconnect, or dissociate feelings that seem "dangerous" to psychic well-being. Engaging this defense mechanism can result in an individual losing touch with his or her true feelings, resulting in a "fragmented self" in proportion to the frequency and degree to which the mechanism is utilized.

127. D: The Health Insurance Portability and Accountability Act of 1996 (HIPAA) applies to all health care providers, health care clearinghouses, and health plan providers. It sets limits on records disclosure and use, provides for individual access to medical records, and establishes the right to receive nots of privacy practices.

128. A: Margaret Mahler most clearly identified with the Object Relations Theory. Rene Spitz and John Bowlby also made substantive contributions to the development of this theory. Heinz Kohut, however, is not directly associated with this theory or its development.

129. A: Employer and supervisor liability accrues under the legal theory of vicarious liability. Although an agency may have liability insurance, it is usually recommended that individual social workers carry their own private coverage. Agency responsibility typically ends at the margins of the scope of the social worker's employment duties (unless agency staff knew in advance of an employee's misconduct and took no protective action). Agency liability continues even off the premises, to the degree the employee's scope of duties extends off the premises.

130. C: This type of behavior is sometimes referred to as "disqualifying communication," meaning that, by words or actions, it disqualifies what one has just said. In the example, the client makes a comment about liking his job and respecting his brother. However, his use of the words "lousy" and "idiot" run counter to the meaning behind those statements and thus disqualify what appears to be the intended message.

131. D: Any information regarding a client that comes to a social worker becomes subject to the rules of confidentiality and privacy of the profession.

132. A: According to Lawrence Kohlberg, an individual fully appreciates the need to conform to social rules and laws at the Conventional Level, stage 4 of moral development.

133. B: While other clients receiving services at the agency may be asked to maintain confidentiality (and this request may even be formalized in group settings) they are not professional bound to ethical standards as are social workers and support staff employed by an agency.

134. B: The responses, according to Pavlovian Classical Conditioning, will be either emitted (voluntary) or reflexive (involuntary) responses.

135. C: 6-12 years old. A "latency-aged" child is one between the ages six and twelve.

136. D: When seeking to overcome problems at the community level or that affect society as a whole, the social worker is functioning as a lobbyist or politician. Effective change at this level typically requires enhanced policy or legislation to align numerous interest groups and resources.

137. C: Because the social worker connects clients to needed resources and services and coordinates the delivery and application of these resources and services, they may be considered a case manager.

138. B: The best response would be to donate the funds to the local Brain Tumor foundation, thanking them for the funds and telling the family where they were sent. This allows the family to see the social worker's gratitude, even while making sure that the funds would be expended in a way that reflects their needs, as well.

139. C: The *NASW Code of Ethics*, most recently updated in 2018, is the best source for the rules, guidelines, and boundaries that define a professional relationship between the social worker and his/her client. While other sources may be informative there is no substitute for studying the NASW Code of Ethics. Policy and procedure manuals and clinical practice texts, in particular, are less likely to provide overarching guidelines of an ethical nature, and instead focus on practical issues for carrying out specific job duties.

140. D: The appropriate response is to cite the professional code of ethics, and clarify that even after a professional relationship ends, socializing is not permitted.

141. A: The best response would be for the social worker to refer the client to another professional promptly, emphasizing the need the client has to remain focused on resolving the important problems involved without any distraction. Feeding the behavior, allowing any level of inappropriate conduct, and confronting the client will only damage the important professional relationship that must exist.

142. B: The process of informing, educating, and reviewing prior to a treatment decision is called informed consent.

143. C: Liberally increasing fees for a client who is particularly well off is not within the ethical behavior outlined by the *NASW Code of Ethics*. Client gouging (charging rates outside of the usual and customary range) is never acceptable.

144. D: The best response for this client would be to involve the client in every aspect that he/she can properly understand, and allow his/her choices to govern where possible. For example, in situations where either a magnetic resonance imaging (MRI) scan or a computed tomography (CT) scan could produce adequate imaging for a requisite test, let the client choose. No one may know, except the client, that he/she has issues with claustrophobia that would make an MRI scan much more burdensome. Thus, asking the client would be essential to supporting his/her right to make independent decisions.

145. A: Social services are never funded via court order (unless from an estate or by some method of litigation—which falls under "personal contributions" as they come from some private individual).

146. B: Under privatization, the government continues paying (but hopes the service will become cheaper to provide). Privatization is undertaken in the hope that the service will be provided less expensively via the private sector, but the government remains the service payer. Issues of accountability sometimes arise once privatization occurs.

147. D: Housing assistance is provided through public housing, subsidized housing, and home loan subsidy programs. There are no "co-op" housing assistance programs based on public assistance.

148. C: The Food Stamps Program is a federally-funded, state administered program that provides purchase vouchers or coupons based on a family's size, income, and resources.

149. A: The Women, Infants, and Children (WIC) program is a federally-funded, state-administered program providing food and assistance to pregnant women, mothers of children up to five months of age (if not breastfeeding), breast-feeding mothers up to 12 months after delivery, and children up to five years of age.

150. B: Meals on wheels is a locally funded program that provides delivery of food to low-income individuals who are unable to leave their home.

Thank You

We at Mometrix would like to extend our heartfelt thanks to you, our friend and patron, for allowing us to play a part in your journey. It is a privilege to serve people from all walks of life who are unified in their commitment to building the best future they can for themselves.

The preparation you devote to these important testing milestones may be the most valuable educational opportunity you have for making a real difference in your life. We encourage you to put your heart into it—that feeling of succeeding, overcoming, and yes, conquering will be well worth the hours you've invested.

We want to hear your story, your struggles and your successes, and if you see any opportunities for us to improve our materials so we can help others even more effectively in the future, please share that with us as well. **The team at Mometrix would be absolutely thrilled to hear from you!** So please, send us an email (support@mometrix.com) and let's stay in touch.

If you feel as though you need additional help, please check out the other resources we offer:

Study Guide: http://MometrixStudyGuides.com/ASWB

Flashcards: http://MometrixFlashcards.com/ASWB